REFUGE *and*
REALITY

REFUGE *and* REALITY

The Blessings of the Temple

JOHN H. GROBERG

ᐰᐰ ®
DESERET
BOOK

Salt Lake City, Utah

Photos courtesy John H. Groberg unless noted otherwise on this page or beside individual photos. All photos used by permission.

Collage on page 130 created by Mike Terry and Thomas Groberg.

Library of Congress Cataloging-in-Publication Data

Groberg, John H., author.
   Refuge and reality : the blessings of the temple / John H. Groberg.
     pages cm
   Includes bibliographical references and index.
   ISBN 978-1-60907-206-3 (hardbound : alk. paper) 1. Temple work (LDS Church) 2. LDS temples. 3. The Church of Jesus Christ of Latter-day Saints—Doctrines. 4. LDS Church—Doctrines. I. Title.
   BX8643.T4G76 2012
   246'.9589332—dc23   2012023486

Printed in the United States of America
Malloy Lithographing Incorporated, Ann Arbor, MI

10 9 8 7 6 5 4 3 2

To MY WIFE, *Jean, and the children God has blessed us with, who are striving to make the temple a bigger part of their lives.*

To MY PARENTS, *Delbert V. and Jennie Holbrook Groberg, who served as president and matron of the Idaho Falls temple from 1975 until 1980. They made the temple a major part of their lives and taught their children to do the same.*

To JEAN'S PARENTS, *Merrill R. and Marie Huber Sabin. They were faithful temple ordinance workers and taught their children to love the temple.*

CONTENTS

ACKNOWLEDGMENTS

With gratitude to my counselors and their wives, Harold W. and Enid Lee Davis and P. Roger and Laura Jo Dunckley DeMordaunt, and to the sealers, ordinance workers, volunteers, staff members, and patrons of the Idaho Falls temple. One could not find more loyal and dedicated helpers anywhere.

And to the thousands who, from everywhere over all

Left to right: Harold W. and Enid L. Davis, John H. and Jean S. Groberg,
and Roger and Laura Jo DeMordaunt.

time, have served in temple presidencies; the hundreds of thousands who have served as ordinance workers and sealers; the millions who have served as temple patrons; and the billions who have received or will yet receive the blessings of the temple.

Chapter 1

INTRODUCTION

We all need a place of refuge from the storms of life. We also need a clear understanding of what is real and eternally important. The temple provides both of these and much more. It is the ultimate refuge from loneliness, uncertainty, darkness, cold, and every other trial and storm of this life. It also teaches us what is real and lasting and brings eternal joy.

Children find love and security in the arms of their parents and peace and safety within the walls of their homes. We are God's children. The temple is His home on earth, and He wants it to be ours as well. He invites all of us to come home to the temple, where we will feel His love and bask in the aura of heavenly light and love that comes from the expanse of eternity.

This book is about individuals who have sought refuge in the temple and found not only safety but understanding and the courage to carry on. Many of these experiences took

1

Image by Tyler Cahoon. Courtesy of The Church of Jesus Christ of Latter-day Saints. Used by permission.

place in the Idaho Falls temple, but similar experiences occur daily in temples throughout the world. As these examples show, I know the temple will bless all who worthily enter and serve therein.

Chapter 2

THE REAL WORLD

When I first began serving as temple president, I often heard people say, "I wish I didn't have to leave the temple, with its peace and quiet, and go back into the real world, with its noise and frustration." I tended to agree with them but for some reason felt uneasy with that thought and prayed to know why.

One day something special happened. I can't say exactly where or how the words or feelings came, but the concept was clear: "That which lasts forever is *real*; that which does not last forever is *not real*. The temple is the *real world*, not this temporal one."

From then on whenever I heard someone say they were sorry to have to leave the temple and go back into the *real world*, I would take them aside and say something like the following:

I understand your feelings, but actually, it is the other way around. You are not leaving the temple and going back into the *real world*, you are leaving the *real world* (the temple) and going back into the *unreal* (temporary) world. Only that which lasts forever is *real*. That which is done in the temple lasts forever; therefore, the *temple* is the *real world*. Most of what we experience "out there," such as sickness, wealth, poverty, fame, etc., lasts for only a short period of time, so it is not the *real world*.

Because you have been in the temple, however, you can take the truths of the *real world* with you as you live in the *temporary world*. As you do, you will see more clearly that which is important (*real*, or eternal) and that which is less important (*unreal*, temporal, or temporary). This view of things will increase your peace, understanding, and joy.

Most would respond, "That is an interesting thought." Later, they would say, "I've been thinking about what you said. I do understand better what is *real* and what is *not real*, and I do feel more peace and joy in my life. Thank you."

I would tell them to thank God, not me, for all truth comes from Him and should be shared with others.

What we do in the temple clearly demonstrates the difference between *real* (eternal) and *unreal* (temporary). In the temple we are reminded of other opposites that we experience in life—opposites such as truth and error, light and darkness, life and death, and especially the difference between Jesus and Satan. That which comes from Jesus is light, lasts forever, and therefore is *real*; that which comes from Satan is darkness, has an end, and in that sense is *not real*. The fact that Satan's temptations come to us and must be dealt with is very real. With the light of the Lord in our lives, we can see that these temptations are based on lies and deceptions; if we resist them, they will fade away into the nothingness they really are.

The viewpoints of this world change quickly. For example, medical science tells us today that something is

good for us, but tomorrow that same thing is bad for us— *Here*
depending on what the latest "experts" say. A song is popular today but mostly forgotten tomorrow. An investment is
good today but a disaster tomorrow. Something that is ac-
ceptable today becomes "politically incorrect" tomorrow. The
best computer today becomes outdated tomorrow. And fickle
fashion changes so rapidly we never know for sure what's currently in vogue.

Any worldly praise or position we might attain here is
temporary. Eternal joy comes only by keeping the laws of *the
real world* as set forth in the temple. Keeping the covenants
made in the temple allows us to experience real peace and
joy in this temporary world even while laying the foundation
for an increase of those precious commodities in eternity. As
President Thomas S. Monson taught, "True joy is found in
holy temples of our Heavenly Father."[1] And that is why we
should not let the cares of this *temporary* world keep us from
the temple and the assurances of the *real world* we find there.
Regular temple attendance therefore provides an answer to
the Savior's prayer: "I pray not that thou shouldst take them
out of the world, but that thou shouldst keep them from the
evil" (John 17:15).

The truths taught in the temple give us an eternal perspective and help keep us from the evil that abounds in the
world. When we see everything through the lens of eternity,
we also see that there is much good and truth in this world
that we can understand if we seek it in the right places and
in the right way.

As we experience the joy that comes from serving in
the temple, our desire increases to be in the temple (the *real
world*) whenever possible. Even when we cannot be in the

The Second Coming, *by Harry Anderson.*

temple, the joy and perspective we enjoy there sustain us and keep us from drowning in the challenges, trials, temptations, and disappointments we inevitably encounter in this *temporary* world.

The fact is, the temple is a bit of heaven on earth. It is where God teaches us to feel, think, act, and speak as we did in heaven before coming here and as we will after leaving here. Truly, the temple is where we become "prepared for the days to come, in the which the Son of Man shall come down in heaven, clothed in the brightness of his glory, to meet the kingdom of God which is set up on the earth" (D&C 65:5).

With the darkness and evil on this earth becoming so stifling that at times it seems hard even to breathe, what a joy it is to go to the temple and inhale deeply of pure light and

Celestial room, Manaus Brazil Temple.

truth! How refreshing to go to a place where darkness and evil are not allowed and where we can see, hear, understand, and embrace *real* principles that never change!

Every day an aura of light flows into the temple from the fountain of eternity. As we enter the temple with a humble and receptive heart, we are bathed in that light and absorb some of it. Thus, when we leave the temple, a portion of that light goes with us and without compulsory means radiates to those about us, bringing increased love, goodness, and joy to all.

In that *real world* we learn that God is our Father, Jesus Christ is His Son, and because of their love and their desire to bless us, we need not fear. They have provided a marvelous plan of salvation; we will be resurrected, and if we are faithful in keeping our temple covenants, we will be redeemed and exalted.

Welcome to the temple.

Welcome to the real world!

Chapter 3

PAY ATTENTION!

Richard grew up in Pocatello, Idaho. His father was not a member of the Church, and his family was only partially active. He did, however, have a loving family, and some friends who were active members took him with them to Primary and other Church activities.

At around age twelve, he received the Aaronic Priesthood and was ordained a deacon. Before long, however, other interests took precedence, and he gradually dropped out of activity. He was still a deacon when he turned seventeen.

Some of his friends invited him to go with them to an open house for the newly completed Idaho Falls temple. World War II had just ended and there was a feeling of better times ahead. Going to a temple open house would be a new experience, so he accepted their invitation.

As they took the tour through the temple, he was impressed with the peace and beauty of everything he saw and felt. The guide was an older gentleman who was not particularly engaging, and Richard found his mind wandering. As his group started up the main staircase to the upper rooms, Richard was not paying much attention to the droning voice of the guide. Suddenly, upon reaching the third step, he clearly heard the admonition: **"Richard! This is important! Pay attention!"**

He was more surprised than alarmed and looked around to see who had spoken to him. He could not detect anyone, but he knew he had heard those words, at least in his mind, so he immediately paid close attention to what the guide was saying. He concentrated on all he was seeing and feeling. Impressed by what he had experienced, Richard determined to also pay closer attention to what his Church leaders asked him to do.

He started attending Church meetings more regularly and was soon ordained a priest and then an elder. He was called on a mission, served faithfully, and continued to listen and obey. He knew the temple and everything about it was important and that he must pay close attention to all of it.

Richard married a faithful and beautiful woman in the Salt Lake Temple. They were blessed with a wonderful family, a meaningful career, and various Church callings. Eventually Richard's father joined the Church, and his parents were sealed to each other and their children were sealed to them in the Idaho Falls temple.

It all began when a young man heeded a prompting he received in the temple to pay attention.

Years later, at the very spot where that prompting had occurred, my wife, Jean, and I were touched and filled with gratitude as Elder Richard G. Scott, now a member of the Quorum of the Twelve Apostles, reverently shared with us this life-changing experience.

Think of the impact—not only on the Scott family but also on the entire world—of one person listening and then

*Richard G. Scott
as a teenager.*

obeying an injunction about the temple! Think of the impact your own hearing and obeying that same injunction can have on you and your family and many others. We might think that we are not of the quality of an Elder Scott and thus not entitled to such an experience. The truth is, however, we are all equally loved by our perfect Father in Heaven and His perfect Son Jesus Christ and are equally able to receive similar inspiration when we are ready to listen and obey.

God's inspiration comes to each of us in slightly different ways because God knows us individually and understands our different capacities, potential, and needs. He guides us and helps us in ways we can understand to fulfill our individual assignments, which, though different from others, are equally important. Our job is to listen, to pay attention, and to obey.

Throughout our lives, each of us has a variety of as-signments, such as son, daughter, husband, wife, mother, fa-ther, home or visiting teacher, missionary, Apostle, Primary leader, Scoutmaster, Relief Society president, Sunday School teacher, or whatever we are called to do. In the scriptures a woman told Jesus how blessed she thought Mary was to be His mother. Jesus responded by saying, "Yea rather, blessed are they that hear the word of God, and keep it" (Luke 11:28). The Savior wasn't minimizing Mary's divine calling but rather reminding each of us to be concerned not with *what* our assignments are but with *how well* we do them.

Our ability to fulfill any assignment is greatly enhanced when we understand the importance of the temple and pay close attention to all that is said and done there. The temple is for redeeming not only the dead but the living as well. All are alive in God, and He is no respecter of persons. Blessings always come from hearing and obeying His word, and His word is never more clear than in the temple.

Each of us can hear the quiet promptings of the Spirit in some way, at some time (usually in many ways and at many times). Those promptings are the voice of the Lord to us. When we truly decide to listen, we will feel a warm stirring within as the Lord communicates with our spirit and affirms to us: *This is important! Pay attention!*

Paying close attention allows us to learn for ourselves the importance of the temple and brings increased joy and confidence. Our thinking the temple is not important to us does not decrease its importance; that way of thinking only decreases our receptiveness to its blessings.

I wish I were able to pay full attention all the time, but I know from personal experience how difficult it is to stay

Painting by James Tissot.

"Could ye not watch with me one hour?" (Matthew 26:40).

constantly alert, especially when our eyes become heavy. When I find myself dozing off, either physically or mentally, I try to remember the Savior asking His disciples to stay awake while He prayed in the Garden of Gethsemane. I'm sure they tried, just as I try, but all of us are vulnerable to the weaknesses of the flesh.

I take solace in the love and compassion Christ demonstrated toward His disciples. When He found them sleeping again the third time, He simply said, "Sleep on" (Mark 14:41).[1] I picture the Savior looking kindly upon them and upon us, much as we might look upon a child, understanding our weakness and still having faith in us. He himself acknowledged that "the spirit indeed is willing, but the flesh is weak" (Matthew 26:41). He knew His disciples were trying. He knew they were in the right place and would ultimately fill their assignments with honor. I'm sure He has that same confidence in each of us.

The accompanying story in song, written about this

event by Liz G. Owen, beautifully captures the feelings not only of that moment but of its meaning to all of us. I hope we will all properly respond to His love and confidence by following His next admonition to them and to us: "Rise up, let us go" (Mark 14:42).

I have known Elder Scott for many years and have been blessed, as have countless others, by his constant willingness to listen to, hear, and obey the word and inspiration of God. In some ways, his experience is singular, but in other ways it is universal. Our Father in Heaven wants to help all of us understand that the temple is important and we must *pay attention* so we can receive the supernal blessings that flow from it.

Regardless of what assignments we have received or may yet be given, I know that we can fill them with honor, with His help. The temple is a major key in receiving this help. There is no limit to the joy and understanding we can receive now and forever as we enter the temple and act upon His admonition to each of us: This is important! Pay attention!

Sleep On

for Low Voice and Piano Accompaniment

Words and Music by
Liz G. Owens

1. They walked with Him to the gar - den that night, then
2. With som - ber heart He re - turned to find His

par - ting at the gate, a friend-ship's fa - vor He did ask of them: Would
friends a - sleep at the gate, twice more the fa - vor He did ask of them: Would

they but watch and pray?
they but watch and pray?

Hours spent in
A - lone, He re -

fer - vent prayer, an - guish and des - pair.
turned to kneel in Geth - sem - a - ne.

O__ Fa - ther let this
The pains of all man -

cup__ pass, This grief, a - lone, so hard to bear.
kind He felt as drops of blood from e - very pore.

I__ shall re - turn to my
When at last His work was com -

15

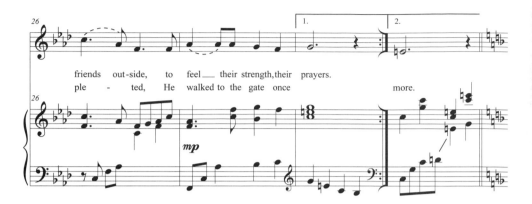

friends out-side, to feel— their strength, their prayers.
ple - ted, He walked to the gate once more.

Then ten-der - ly, He looked u-pon His wea - ry friends. And, through si-lent tears He

said: "Sleep On and take your rest, my friends. Sleep

16

On,_____ the hour is nigh at __ hand. Sleep On,_____ my peace and

love I send. Sleep On.

And when I am bur - dened, faint,___ or wea -

ry, I___ think of my Sa - vior, and I can al - most

see how ten - der ly, He looks u - pon my wea - ri - ness,

dolce

and, through smi - ling eyes He says: "Sleep On,____ and take your

tranquillo

rest, my friend. Sleep on,_____ you can en - dure to the end. I

know_____ your heart, I un - der stand. Sleep On."

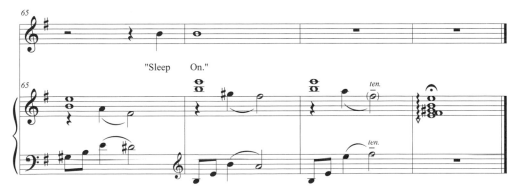

"Sleep On."

19

Chapter 4

ELUSIVE ANSWERS

A man said his bishop and stake president had encouraged him to come to the temple and if possible visit with me. This good brother told me he had some serious challenges and had been coming to the temple regularly, seeking understanding and strength, but so far they had eluded him. He asked, "What am I doing wrong? I thought by coming here more often I would receive more help and answers. Why am I still confused?"

I encouraged him to continue coming to the temple and striving to increase his faith in the Lord. I bore my testimony that in the Lord's time and way, he and others would receive the inspiration and help they needed. He humbly accepted that counsel and promised to continue coming to the temple and to keep praying for help.

As he stood to leave, I felt impressed to say, "The next time you come to the temple, try not to concentrate on your challenges but concentrate instead on the challenges of the person you are representing. Ponder on such things as, When and where did he live? What kinds of challenges did he have?

What was his family like? What did he do for a living? What was his daily life like?

"As you do this, you will understand that many of his challenges are similar to yours and maybe even harder. Concentrate on each person you represent, and pray for him to understand and accept what the Savior has done for him. That person likely had many challenges while here and perhaps still has many. Through the Savior and the temple you are his best hope.

"The Lord smiles on those who use their time and effort to help others. As you concentrate on the person you are representing and on his challenges more than on your own, I believe solutions to your challenges will become more clear."

He thanked me for the suggestion and promised he would do so.

Many months later I attended a stake conference where a man was sustained as a member of the high council and asked to bear his testimony. As he came to the stand to respond, he passed in front of me, and I recognized him as the same man who had spoken with me in the temple much earlier. He smiled and gave a brief nod of acknowledgment.

He stood tall and confident and spoke beautifully and powerfully. He expressed his love for the Lord, his wife, his family, and all the good people who had helped him and his family overcome their recent challenges. He testified that the Lord hears and answers prayers in the way and at the time that is best for us. He bore testimony of the importance of attending the temple and truly working for others by putting forth effort both physically and spiritually on their behalf. He said he knew personally how deeply these people needed and appreciated our help. He encouraged everyone going to the temple not to just act as a proxy but to actually put forth spiritual effort to try to help those they represent.

Then he said, "I have two questions for you. I have thought a lot about these questions and would like you to ponder them seriously. First, Why should the Lord bless us if that blessing simply stops with us? Second, Why should He not bless us if He knows we will use that blessing to help others?" His sincerity and the powerful effect of those questions and his testimony were felt by everyone present. He had learned an important truth and had effectively shared it with others. As he returned to his seat, we simply exchanged smiles, both grateful for the important truths we had learned and been able to share with others.

Receiving impressions from the Lord and following them becomes its own reward, and we don't need outside confirmation. Can you think of a greater blessing than knowing that the Lord trusts you enough to give you an impression that can help someone else? What a blessing to know that the Lord trusts you enough to allow you to help someone else, as his or her proxy in the temple! We should not hope for praise for acting as a conduit for the Lord's truths but rather feel to express gratitude for the privilege of being such a conduit.

I have come to know that we learn much more of what is important when we concentrate on helping others than when we concentrate on our own challenges. When we use the blessings the Lord has given us primarily for our own benefit, we close doors to eternal understanding and progress. When we energetically seek to use the blessings the Lord has given us to help others, we open many more doors of heaven, and there is no limit to what we can understand and do.

I know that as we put forth more effort to help others,

we gain deeper understanding of where we fit in this big and expanding universe, where we fit in our eternal families, and where we fit as one who wants to help the Lord "bring to pass the immortality and eternal life of man" (Moses 1:39). The temple is a place where we can more effectively be a useful part of this great eternal round of helping others.

This man had learned where he fit in. Because of his humble but sincere service to others, the answers to his questions no longer eluded him. He had learned the truth of King Benjamin's assurance that "when ye are in the service of your fellow beings ye are only in the service of your God" (Mosiah 2:17), and in return for that service to others, the man had himself been greatly blessed.

Chapter 5

WHAT'S WRONG WITH ME?

After a stake conference at which I spoke on the blessings of regular temple attendance, a young woman named Linda asked if she could visit me in my office.

When we later met, she said she was confused because she believed everything I had said at the conference but so far none of the promised blessings had come to her and she wondered why. She explained that she had grown up in the Church, served a full-time mission, graduated from college, and had been teaching for several years at a local grade school. She presently served as a Primary leader, participated actively in her ward, and attended the temple regularly.

She then recounted the promises I had made to all who, with an honest heart and sincere desire to help others, attend the temple regularly. I was impressed by the accuracy of her notes and her memory. She reminded me that I had promised the congregation that the Lord would inspire them on how to overcome their personal challenges and thus receive joy and fulfillment. She quoted me as saying, "At times that help might come by having our challenges put into an eternal perspective that we can understand and live with, in patience and hope." She then reviewed several other promises I had made and asked if they were valid.

I responded, "You take good notes and have a great memory. Those are things I said, and those are things I believe."

"I want to believe them also," she replied. "I have been attending the temple regularly for several years, but I am still single, and the joy of a family I have hoped and prayed for has not come. In fact, my challenges seem to be increasing. Since I believe you are telling the truth, I want to ask, What's wrong with me?"

Seldom have I been at a greater loss for words or felt a greater need for divine inspiration. She was an attractive young woman, maybe not beautiful as the world defines that term, but she was attractive and filled with goodness. What would God have me say to her?

It would be nice to have a ready answer for everyone on every subject, but some situations seem to be beyond our current ability to comprehend or articulate. That is how I felt as I looked into her faithful, waiting eyes. Slowly thoughts began to form in my mind, and I asked, "Does your coming to the temple make you feel better or worse?"

"Of course I feel better," she replied. "I love the temple. It is not the temple I am questioning—it's me! There is nothing wrong with the temple, just with me. What is it?"

A burst of inspiration came, and I replied, "Linda, there is nothing wrong with you, at least not in the way you are thinking. Your bishop and stake president have found you worthy to enter the Lord's house. God loves you. He is pleased with your desires to help others. He knows your heart. He has blessed you greatly and will continue to do so. No one can have a greater blessing than to *know* that they are worthy to enter the temple—to *know* that they are a son or daughter of God—to *know* that He loves them—to know that He has sent His Beloved Son to suffer and die for them—to *know* that through faith in Him and obedience to Him, they can enjoy eternal life. Do you believe these things?"

"Yes, I do!"

"Linda, I testify that God knows you and loves you fully. He knows your feelings and frustrations and everything you are going through. He is by your side, closer than you can imagine. He is pleased with your faithfulness and your desire and willingness to serve others in the temple and elsewhere.

"Time as we know it is a mortal measure and does not exist with God (see Alma 40:8). He has decreed that certain things need to be accomplished in mortality; however, the main thing we must accomplish while here is to develop deep faith in and love for our Savior. As we patiently persist in this faith and love to the end of our mortal lives, it does not matter whether certain events that were beyond our control came to pass in mortality. God's promise to the faithful is that everything necessary for eternal life will happen some-time, somewhere, someway. On the other hand, if we are not faithful here and do not increase our love, our patience, and our faith in God, it doesn't matter what things may have oc-curred here; they lose their value because all eternal blessings are based on faithfulness."

I asked her to stay close to her parents and to follow the counsel of her bishop, as she had her mission president. I re-minded her to study the scriptures, pray, and serve whenever and wherever called. I also asked her to read her patriarchal blessing over and over again and do everything in her power

Courtesy Intellectual Reserve, Inc.

to be worthy of those promises being fulfilled. I promised her that as she faithfully did these things, she could then "stand . . . still, and see the salvation of the Lord" (2 Chronicles 20:17). I concluded by saying that she likely had been told many times before to be faithful and patient, but I needed to say it again, for that is what the Lord impressed me to say.

She looked down for what seemed a long time. A tear ran down her cheek, and I sensed a slight tremor as she closed her eyes. Finally she looked up, smiled, and said softly, "Thank you. I do know what is right. I do want to be faithful and obedient. I love the temple. I know it is where I should be. I look forward to helping others—in school, in Primary, in the temple, and in many other places. It is just that I . . . I thought things would be different. I have to confess that sometimes I just get tired of waiting. Thank you for assuring me that all the 'events' needed for my eternal joy will happen at some point if I continue faithful. I believe this. I promise you I will continue to be patient and faithful and keep helping and hoping. Please understand that sometimes it is just plain hard to wait."

I assured her that I understood. I also reminded her that each of us faces our own individual challenges, which God customizes for our personal growth.

"Don't worry," she said. "I'll be all right. It is good to know that there is nothing major wrong with me and that God still loves me. Thanks for listening."

She smiled, expressed her love and appreciation, and left.

I was deeply moved by the goodness, faithfulness, and testimony of this wonderful daughter of God and felt impressed to say an extra prayer for her and others in similar circumstances. As I did, I began to think about her question and her response to my words and started wondering how many other faithful daughters of God are patiently (and sometimes not so patiently) waiting for the "salvation of the Lord." I had the feeling that there are many such on both sides of the veil and wondered what more I could do to help. I realized that many young men and young women have challenges that I am not aware of, but God is. Ultimately, all fear and uncertainty are resolved by exercising more faith in the Savior. He is the only One through whom we can overcome all things.

I knew I didn't have all the answers, but I also knew that the ultimate answer for all of us who struggle with these and other challenges is having greater faith and trust in the Lord Jesus Christ. As we actually trust Him and take the needed steps—sometimes in semidarkness—He will help us break free of the chains of fear and uncertainty and move us over the chasm of doubt to the bright light and joy of faith fulfilled. There is nothing wrong with any of us that more and deeper faith in the Lord Jesus Christ won't overcome.

I sensed the subtlety of Satan in sowing doubts in our hearts by whispering that we are unprepared or unworthy or unlikeable and therefore have no hope of entering into marriage and having a family. I knew the best thing I could do is to increase my own faith in God and help others to do likewise. Going to the temple regularly increases our faith in the Lord, exposes Satan for what he is and his lies for what they are, and gives us strength to do what is right.

I thanked God for helping this beautiful sister increase her faith and patience and love and obedience. I continued to plead for her and for countless others similar to her—and with equal fervor for their young men counterparts. As I prayed, I began to feel more deeply the love and assurance from an all-wise and all-powerful Heavenly Father that all will ultimately be well with all who are faithful.

For a moment I caught a glimpse of thousands, millions, even an innumerable host of men and women whose mortal lives were cut short through war, famine, or disease, or who in mortality never knew about Jesus or the gospel or the temple, or who never understood the eternal meaning and importance of families. I seemed to see many faithful men and women in the spirit world explaining these truths to others, teaching and testifying and helping them so they can receive every needful blessing. I knew there would be no shortage of companions and families for those who are faithful.

I felt much as Joseph Smith must have felt when he saw in vision his brother Alvin in the celestial kingdom, even though Alvin had not been baptized nor married before he died (see D&C 137) or as President Joseph F. Smith must have felt when he saw all that was being done and would yet be done for those who did not have the opportunity for these ordinances here in mortality (see D&C 138). I understood with even deeper conviction the importance of the work being done in the temples. I thanked the Lord for the assurance that all the Lindas and all the Alvins who ever have or ever will live here will be all right as long as they remain faithful.

Chapter 6

CAROL

The enthusiasm and goodness of young people who come to the temple to do baptisms is marvelous to observe. You can feel God's love for them and His confidence in them. One late afternoon I met with a large group of youth from a rural ward. As I looked into their fresh bright faces, I knew I was looking into the faces of the hope of the Church and the world. And as I spoke to them and bore my testimony, I felt something extra special about this particular group.

When I finished speaking to them, their bishop dismissed them to change into their baptismal clothes, and I started to return upstairs. I felt prompted to turn around. It appeared that everyone had left; however, from the corner of my eye I noticed a young girl who was hanging back, partially hidden behind a door casing. She was looking down, and I could tell she did not want to be noticed. But I felt impressed to go back, shake her hand, and ask her name. "Carol," she timidly replied. Then I noticed that one side of her face was some-what disfigured—perhaps from an accident or a birth defect.

A feeling of deep compassion came over me, and I was led to say, "Carol, God loves you. He is happy that you have

chosen to come to the temple tonight. He is pleased that you want to help other people by doing important things for them, things that they cannot do for themselves. The Savior Himself came to earth to do important things for us—things that we could not do for ourselves. He unselfishly laid down His life for you, for me, and for everyone in the whole world so we could all have a chance to progress and have eternal joy."

I sensed goodness radiating from her and also felt to tell her, "Carol, I know that Jesus is our Savior, and tonight you are His special helper by being a Savior on Mount Zion with Him. He loves you and is grateful that you have come to the temple to help others so that they might have a chance for progress and joy."

She looked up a little, and I continued. "Carol, there is something else the Lord wants you to know. He wants you to know that He understands what it is like to have a marred appearance. The prophet Isaiah said of Christ: 'his visage [appearance] was so marred more than any man . . . He is despised and rejected of men; a man of sorrows, and acquainted with grief: and we hid as it were our faces from him' (Isaiah 52:14; 53:3–5). He understands your situation, and He loves you for coming here. Be assured, He looks not on your outward appearance but on your heart. When He looked at your heart tonight, He saw beauty and goodness. Others might see something else, but not the Savior. Remember, it is not what others think of you that counts but what God thinks of you. He wants you to know that to Him you are beautiful—every bit of you. He wants you to know that He loves you, every bit of you. He wants you to know that every blessing available to any of His daughters is available to you. He wants you to know that because of your faithfulness and your desire to help others, every needful blessing will eventually be yours."

She smiled but didn't say anything, so I told her to hurry and catch up with the others. As she moved quietly down the hall toward the changing room, I noticed that she was smiling a little, holding her head a little higher, and walking with a little more confidence in her step.

A few days later Carol's bishop called. He told me what a blessing it had been for the youth of his ward to be in the temple and to do baptisms for the dead. He told me that from his experience, having the youth and other ward members in the temple blesses them more than almost anything else he knows of. Then he said, "I don't know what you said to Carol, but thanks for whatever it was. Ever since our trip to the temple she has been happier, more friendly, more confident, and she is smiling more than I have seen her do in years."

I commended him for the wonderful youth of his ward,

and I told him that Carol was a special person and the Lord had in fact given her a special message. I reminded him that all who come to the temple and unselfishly give of their time and effort to do work for those who cannot do it for themselves could receive that same message and encouraged him to keep as a top priority the spiritual and physical welfare of the youth. He assured me he would, and we concluded our conversation.

After hanging up the phone, I began to think of what a blessing it would be if everyone understood the message God had given Carol that evening. What a blessing to know that His concern is not with our outward appearance or circumstances but with our hearts and our desire to help others. Understanding that basic truth lets us know what we need to do to be happy and have joy in our lives. We may not be able to determine our outward appearance or circumstances, but we can control our hearts and our desires, and that is what God sees and understands and knows to be our true selves.

The Lord's message to Carol that evening is in fact a message to all of us. Regardless of our current challenges, we can always find ways to help someone else. God doesn't want us to be sad or hang back or keep our heads down. He wants us to be happy by helping others. He wants us to smile and look up and move forward with confidence in Him. Carol did that, and so can we!

Chapter 7

CHOICES

One afternoon a shift coordinator came to my office and said, "I'm sorry that some of the sessions on my shift were not very well attended. I don't know what I am doing wrong. Can you help me understand what more I should do?"

I looked into his humble, inquiring eyes, and a strong impression came to me. I said, "Sit down for a moment. The Lord wants you to know that He loves you, that He is pleased with your efforts, and that you should not feel guilty for the small attendance but rather be grateful for those who do come. He wants you to rejoice in the privilege you have to serve in His house and not be sorrowful for things that are beyond your control."

He looked up and with a combination of joy and wonder said, "Really?"

"Really," I replied. His eyes became a bit tearful as I continued, "The Lord wants you to understand that He invites, not assigns, people to come to Him in His temple. You have accepted His invitation to come to Him here. Others must make their own decision whether to accept His invitation or not.

"Blessings come according to the choices we make. You have chosen well and will receive the joy that comes from that choice. Yes, we feel sorrow for those who make choices that will not bring them lasting joy but remember, it is their choice. There are things over which we have control, and there are things over which we do not have control. The best way to help others experience the joy that comes from correct choices is to radiate the joy we receive from making those choices, such as serving here in the temple."

He said that he really was grateful for the privilege of serving in the Lord's house and would try to serve even better by showing more joy and less sorrow. I commended him on the good choices he had made in his life and testified that he and those around him would be blessed for his doing so.

I was touched by the humility of this man, by his genuine desire to serve more faithfully, and by his gratitude for the truths that had become more clear to him. As I thought of him and the impressions I had received, I began to wonder if I was doing *my* full duty and radiating the joy I should for the privilege of serving in the Lord's house. I knew that one of my duties was to express love and appreciation to the workers and patrons who were voluntarily coming so faithfully to the temple. I resolved to spend more time thanking all who came. As I did so and expressed God's love for their accepting His invitation, I felt impressed to promise them greater spiritual strength, understanding, and love as a consequence of their service. I had the distinct feeling that many from the other side were also adding their love, gratitude, and encouragement to those patrons and workers.

King Benjamin explained that when we show our love and gratitude to God by doing what He asks, He immediately

Calling of the Fishermen, by Harry Anderson. Courtesy Intellectual Reserve, Inc.

We each must choose whether to follow Him.

blesses us, so we are still in His debt and always will be. I was amazed at the assurance that God loves us enough to continue to give and give and give, no matter how deeply in debt we get to Him! The best (and maybe the only) "payment" we can make is to increase our effort to love and help others in every way we can. What a blessing the temple is in providing us an opportunity to do this!

The Three Nephites asked permission to remain in mortality until the Savior's Second Coming to spend that time in helping others come unto Christ. In response to their request, they were promised they would "not have pain while ye shall dwell in the flesh, neither sorrow save it be for the sins of the world" (3 Nephi 28:9). They and all of us will feel sorrow for those (sometimes including ourselves) who choose not to accept the Lord's invitation to come unto Him, especially in His house. We, just like the Three Nephites, have the duty to preach, testify, and encourage in every way we can, of course, but we must remember that the choice to come unto Him and to the temple is ultimately the personal choice of each individual.

President Thomas S. Monson has pointed out, "When we truly understand and appreciate the purpose for which temples are built, we will not want to be deprived of the blessings of coming herein."[1]

I have learned that as we shape our actions and our attitudes to fit the template of the temple, great blessings flow into our lives. We better understand how to help those around us, especially our own families. We see more clearly our true role as God's stewards. We feel His guidance and direction in showing us how to use our agency, health, and ability to move and communicate, as well as the time, talents, and everything else He has given us to bless others and build His kingdom (see D&C 104:12–18). In short, we become more Christlike and experience more joy.

As a result of my visit with this concerned temple worker, I resolved to spend more time and energy serving in His house and thanking others for doing the same, and to spend less time and energy worrying about whether or not others accept His invitation to come and receive His blessings. Any time and energy we spend worrying about the choices other people make that are beyond our control is not only wasted but takes away from the time and energy we could be using to better serve others.

I know that sorrow is real and is felt by all of us—even the Savior. I also know that the sorrow we have the most control over is the personal sorrow we feel when we don't accept the Lord's invitation to do our duty and help others as we should. We can turn this type of sorrow to joy, simply by putting forth more effort to help others. As we do, we move closer to the Savior and experience more joy and more understanding of how to better help others. All movement toward the Savior is a change for the better, and since repentance means a change for the better, it is easy to see why He directs us to "say nothing but repentance unto this generation," including ourselves (D&C 11:9).

After that day, each time I saw that particular coordinator, he would whisper, "I had many wonderful people attend my sessions today. How grateful I am that they made the choice to come to the temple and let me share in the joy they are bringing to their lives and the lives of others."

Chapter 8

MAKING THE TEMPLE A BIGGER PART OF LIFE

One day a patron asked me when a particular brother was scheduled to be on duty in the initiatory area. I asked why he wanted to know. The man said he had recently been there when this particular ordinance worker had been serving as one of the officiators and had never felt such a wonderful spirit. The patron knew it didn't matter who performed the ordinance but said, "I can't really explain how, but when this worker, who is blind, performed the ordinance, I just felt something special. It was as though being physically blind, he could spiritually see more and conveyed the significance of these ordinances in a way I had never felt or understood before."

After the patron left, I thought back on the circumstance surrounding the calling of that particular ordinance worker. He desired to work in the temple but felt his being blind would preclude his doing so. His bishop felt impressed to recommend him, however, and after being interviewed by the temple presidency, the blind brother was set apart as an ordinance worker.

At first, he and the other workers on his shift were

hesitant as to how to proceed, but over time everything fell into place, and soon he was an integral part of that shift. Before long he had memorized every square inch of the temple and could get around about as well as anyone—and better than some. He put his whole heart and soul into his calling and became fully engaged. There were some things he could not do, but there were many things he could do, and he did them very well.

He made the temple a bigger part of his life, and in doing so he not only experienced increased joy himself but also helped others feel more joy. From his example it was easy to see that despite the physical limitations we may have, there are still many significant ways we can serve. If we are humble and faithful, the Lord more than compensates for our limitations.

A wonderful widowed sister who was confined to a motorized chair by her multiple sclerosis was by inspiration called as an ordinance worker. What a blessing this proved to be to her and to all she serves.

I wondered if some physical limitations may actually be blessings in disguise, which allow the Lord to give us additional spiritual awareness that we might not otherwise achieve. It may be that if we were to lose (or get rid of) more things, we might be able to see eternal things more clearly. As we see that our recommends are current and see that we attend the temple more often and see that we pay closer attention to all that is said and done there, our spiritual eyes will comprehend much more.

I testify that anyone who sincerely and consistently makes the temple a bigger part of his or her life will experience an increase in understanding, happiness, calmness, direction, testimony, patience, faith, and every other component of eternal joy. That is true regardless of health or wealth or other temporal circumstance or limitations. I have lived and worked in many countries, among people speaking different languages and living in a vast variety of economic, political, health, and cultural circumstances, yet in all cases, whenever individuals, communities, or countries make the temple a bigger part of their lives in any way, they always experience increased joy.

God is the source of eternal joy and has designated the temple as the place for His children to receive the teachings, ordinances, and power that enable them to experience that joy in its fulness. God loves all of His children equally, and because the laws for receiving eternal joy are both universal and eternal, He invites everyone to come to Him in His temple and receive those blessings. That is certainly one of the reasons He inspires His prophets to say such things as, "It would be the deepest desire of my heart to have every member of the Church be temple worthy."[1]

Because so much of our happiness now and throughout eternity depends on our relationship to the temple, one of the most important questions you can ask is, How can I make the temple a bigger part of my life?

The answer is to begin wherever you are and earnestly move toward the Lord and His temple. If you are not involved in the Church, either by not being a member or not being fully active, you can begin where you are. Start by simply looking at the temple. You can walk around its grounds, contemplate the beauty of the building, and ask God how you can make this bit of heaven a bigger part of your life. You can consciously think about your forebears and in so doing turn your heart to your fathers (see Malachi 4:6) by doing family history research. When a temple open house is held, you can attend and view firsthand the interior of the Lord's house with its beautiful appointments and lovely furnishings. You can ask member friends to tell you more about the temple. You can ask for literature about temples. You can go to a Church Visitors' Center, either physically or online. You can ask missionaries to explain the purpose of temples to you. All of this can be done at your leisure and without any pressure by going to www.lds.org, clicking on Menu and then Temples.

No matter who you are, where you live, or what your circumstances are, if you desire to experience more purpose and joy in life, you can do so by acquiring a better understanding of the Lord and His temple. If you are willing to take the needed steps, the Lord will bless you.

For example, while serving as a bishop in Idaho Falls many years ago, I became acquainted with a young man who had moved there from the Midwest for a job. He spent his first night at a motel across the river from the Idaho Falls temple. He was fascinated by the beauty of the temple and its reflection in the river. He said it reminded him of a wedding cake.

He later heard many negative comments about the Church from some fellow workers but continued to feel that there was something good about that beautiful structure. He persisted in asking questions about the building and how he could go inside. Soon the missionaries were teaching him, and before long he joined the Church. He stayed active and eventually married a lovely young lady in that temple by the river. They have a wonderful family, have served in many important ways, and continue to experience ever-increasing joy.

Idaho Falls temple at night from across the Snake River.

There is a place for everyone in the temple. God constantly beckons and invites all of us to come unto Him in His temple where He can share His light with us. A woman who moved into a house very close to the temple told us, "I don't live in the 'shadow' of the temple, as some say. I live in the 'light' of the temple." The distinction she made is valid. Understanding that the temple is a source of light, she lived her life accordingly and received great blessings.

If we consider ourselves active in the Church but still don't feel the joy we would like to, we need to redouble our efforts to make the temple an even bigger part of our life.

When persecution was raging in Nauvoo, the Prophet Joseph Smith was forced into hiding. It wouldn't be long before he and his brother Hyrum would be martyred and the Saints would be driven from Nauvoo and forced to abandon

Joseph Smith before the Nauvoo
Temple, *by Dale Kilbourn.*

the temple they had been building. To help prepare them for these trials, the Lord inspired the Prophet to write these words to the Saints in Nauvoo:

"And again, verily thus saith the Lord: Let the work of my temple . . . be *redoubled.* . . . And if they persecute you [or if it is hard for you to make the temple a bigger part of your life], so persecuted they the prophets and righteous men that were before you. [It was hard for them also, but they did it.] For all this there is a reward in heaven [then and now]" (D&C 127:4; emphasis added).

The Saints obeyed the Prophet and made the temple a bigger, even a huge, part of their lives. Because they did, they were later on better able to endure the tasks of crossing the plains and establishing Zion in "the top of the mountains" (Isaiah 2:2). As we do the same, we will be better able to make it here and hereafter.

President Thomas S. Monson has said, "Those who understand the eternal blessings which come from the temple know that no sacrifice is too great, no price too heavy, no struggle too difficult in order to receive those blessings."[2]

We all have different circumstances—some live far from temples, some have serious health challenges, some have young families, some are caring for older relatives, some are young (in age, testimony, or experience), and some do not yet comprehend the importance of temples. If we try, however, all of us can in some way make the temple a bigger part of our lives, thus enabling us to receive added strength to meet the challenges of life.

President Gordon B. Hinckley promised: "Every man or woman who goes to the temple comes out of that building a better man or woman than he or she was when entering into it."[3] I confess I don't know *how* it happens; I just know that it happens. I have observed over and over again that as we attend the temple regularly, little by little, we see more clearly, act more in accordance with eternal temple principles, and receive more joy.

Whether we are presently a member of His Church or not, active or not, living here or living beyond the veil, whenever and however we make the temple a bigger part of our life, we will experience increased joy. And when we make the fulness of the temple the full pattern of our lives, we will experience a fulness of joy!

Chapter 9

CELEBRATIONS

There was a contagious enthusiasm in the air when I arrived at the temple one morning. Several of the workers excitedly told me, "It's Brother Baker's ninety-sixth birthday today! He is doing work for his family. He did some baptisms and other ordinances earlier and is now participating in an endowment session. What a man! What a way to celebrate a birthday!"

I had not yet met Brother Baker but was impressed by the feelings of love and admiration so many ordinance workers had for him. When I said I would like to meet him, the workers said he was doing sessions until noon but would come to the cafeteria for lunch. They had prepared a surprise for him, and I could meet and visit with him then.

Noon came, and I had a wonderful visit with Brother Baker. He was a small, wiry man with piercing eyes and a quick sense of humor. After we finished eating lunch, several of the workers brought in a birthday cake. It was obvious that he felt the same affection for the workers that they felt for him. When he blew out the candles someone jokingly said, "Now you can go out and really celebrate your birthday."

Brother Lloyd Baker
from Wyoming.

Brother Baker quickly responded, "I'm celebrating it right now! There is no better way to celebrate my birthday than coming to a place where I can feel close to my whole family and help them in eternally important ways. That's the best gift I can think of." With a twinkle in his eye he looked at those around him and said, "When you get a little older, you'll understand."

He thanked us for lunch and said he needed to hurry to catch the next two sessions before having to return home. "I would stay longer, but the silly sheriff from my hometown in Wyoming won't let me drive after dark." I was amazed when I learned that he often drove himself to and from the temple. I was also impressed at how good his eyesight, hearing, mental alertness, and general health were.

Just before he left the temple, I visited with him again.

With his engaging smile, he lamented the fact that he had just enough time to make it home before the sheriff's silly curfew fell. His final words were, "What a great birthday this has been!" I had a strong feeling that such faith would be rewarded even in unexpected ways.

I returned to my office just as Sister Groberg stepped in to share an experience she had had while I was visiting with Brother Baker. There had been a young woman standing in the hallway near the sisters' dressing area who seemed a little unsure of which way to go, so Jean asked if she needed help. "Oh, yes, I am a little confused. This is my first time back to the temple since we were married." As they walked together to the proper place, Jean asked the woman, "And how long have you been married?"

Her smile seemed to light up the entire room as she answered, "Oh, for one whole week! This is our one-week anniversary! When we were married, we were counseled to come back to the temple as often as we could, so my husband and I decided to come every week as long as we could, so here we are. Isn't marriage wonderful? Isn't the temple wonderful? We are so happy and so grateful for the temple. Aren't anniversaries great?"

Just as we finished this conversation, my secretary reminded me that it was time to go to the chapel and meet with a large group who had come to the temple as part of their family reunion. We had a wonderful meeting with this family, and as they left for their endowment session I could feel their happiness at being together in the temple. A few minutes later, another large family came to do work for some of their deceased relatives. What joy both of these families felt as they celebrated being part of an eternal family by helping

Photo of Craig and Gayle Teuscher. Courtesy Don Busath.

and feeling closer to each other as well as to members of their family on the other side of the veil.

A little later in the day I officiated at the marriage of a young couple, who along with their families and friends filled the sealing room with a celestial radiance and a perfect brightness of hope that was remarkable. As I witnessed this new family being brought into existence, I marveled at the wonderful and blessed way this couple had chosen to begin their lives together. I knew that as they kept their family rooted in the teachings of the temple, one day their children and grandchildren and on forever could and would reunite in the temple to celebrate their eternal families (see 2 Nephi 31:20).

Shortly thereafter we experienced another type of reunion. It was September 23, the anniversary of the day

President George Albert Smith dedicated the Idaho Falls Idaho Temple in 1945. We had scheduled a special chapel meeting to be followed by an endowment session for all those who had attended the original open house or dedication of the Idaho Falls temple.

Most of those who were present in 1945 were now living on the other side of the veil, so we were not sure how many would physically attend. When the hour arrived, however, the chapel and the assembly room were both filled to capacity with grateful patrons. Some were in wheelchairs or had walkers or oxygen tanks, and many had younger family members or friends assisting them. But the feeling of joy, gratitude, and faith seemed just as strong, if not stronger, than it was more than sixty years before.

The next two sessions were filled with mostly older folks, but more important, they were filled with persons who recalled pleasant memories and had both a desire to help others and a continued dedication to serve the Lord whenever, wherever, however, and forever. Many expressed their assurance that this anniversary and this work were being recognized "over there" as well as "here." Several told me of the closeness they felt with departed loved ones and suggested that many of us "younger folks" might not yet fully understand this.

Before I left the temple, I took some time in my office to thank the Lord for all those faithful people. As I reviewed the experiences I had enjoyed with families and birthdays and anniversaries, I was made aware again of what a long time eternity is. Mortality is part of eternity, so we should learn to get along with and help *all* of our family, *all* of the time, both here and there. We must learn to include one another and help all those here who don't yet understand the gospel, as well as all those who left mortality without receiving the blessings of the gospel. I believe our effectiveness in providing this help increases or decreases as our dedication to the Lord and His temple increases or decreases.

Families are the building blocks of eternity and are formed, sealed, and proceed on forever through the temple. The phrases "born again," "born anew," "second birth," "born in the covenant," and "born unto eternal life" are more than just symbolic phrases. They are real events. We are all part of God's eternal family, and He wants us to be together forever. Life, death, birth, adoption, sealing, family, temple—all these events and institutions are truly meaningful only in the context of eternity.

In this sense, temples are about family reunions and about celebrating various kinds of births. New members come into our family circle in mortality through the adoptions, births, and marriages we celebrate here. We should remember that these same events are equally significant and meaningful to those of our family who are over there. As we celebrate all of these events we should be very grateful for the opportunity to go to the temple to help bring these blessings to *all* the members of our family.

Since family ties are the essence of eternal life, is it any wonder that Satan tries to keep us from the temple and tries to keep us from having families? No wonder he works so hard to convince us that "extra" children are a burden or a threat to our personal growth, financial well-being, social life, or recreational pleasures when in fact the opposite is true. In the temple, Satan, the great deceiver, is unmasked. There we are taught to become more, not less, involved with our

Courtesy Jane Garner

John and Jean Groberg family reunion.

families, both those here and those beyond the veil. As we become more oriented toward the temple and eternity and God and away from the world and mortal time and Satan, we begin to truly understand the completeness of life.

There is something magical about family reunions both here and there. They remind us of who we are and where we belong. Our joy in reunions increases as we are able to give a good account of ourselves and our place in our eternal family. Birthdays, anniversaries, reunions, dedications, remembrances—especially in the temple—are all part of God's plan to help us experience the joy in our families He designed for us both now and forever.

As I reflected on these truths, I recalled the sparkle and enthusiasm of a ninety-six-year-old patron, the excitement and enthusiasm of a couple married one whole week, the joy of families being united on many levels, and the patience and endurance of faithful people filled with precious memories. Yes, the temple and indeed life itself are really about celebrating families.

Chapter 10

THE GREATEST
TEACHER

One evening a bishop asked if he, the Relief Society president, and another sister from their ward who had some concerns could meet with me. They had just finished an endowment session, and this sister had told the bishop and the Relief Society president that she did not understand or agree with some things she had seen and heard and so had decided she would not come back to the temple. They had tried to assure her that over time she would understand more and feel better, but she was adamant and insisted she wasn't coming back. They didn't want her to leave the temple while harboring those feelings, so they asked if she would be willing to visit with the temple president. She said she would, so here they were.

I knew that the endowment is understood only through personal revelation, which is God's Spirit speaking to our spirit, so if she was not sufficiently humble to be able to receive this revelation, no amount of other explanations would resolve her concerns—whatever they might be. I prayed for inspiration. Rather than ask what her concerns were, I felt impressed to ask if she would tell me a little about herself.

She was happy to do so and proceeded to explain that she had been married in the temple many years before but that she and her husband had never gone back to the temple. They had not stayed active in the Church nor had children but had managed to accumulate lots of "toys." They thought these would bring them happiness, but they never had. After being married for several years, they had gone through a difficult divorce, and she was left with bitter feelings toward her former husband and indifference toward the Church and the covenants she had made.

She eventually moved to a new neighborhood where she was befriended by several sisters. She appreciated their friendship and at their invitation began attending church with them. She enjoyed the association with ward members and became quite active. After a while her friends encouraged her to go to the temple with them. She was hesitant but talked to her bishop, who suggested she take the temple preparation lessons. After a few months of study and continuing activity, she felt she was ready to go to the temple and had come with the Relief Society president, the bishop, and a few others from the ward that evening.

She told me she remembered hardly anything from when she had been sealed to her husband years before. But during the presentation of the endowment this evening, she had heard some things she didn't agree with and had decided she didn't want to return.

At that point, the woman turned to her bishop and Relief Society president and said she still loved them and would keep coming to church but probably not to the temple.

There was a moment of awkward silence. Suddenly I had

an impression and asked, "You are a schoolteacher, aren't you?"

She was surprised because that had not been mentioned, but she responded, "Yes, I am. How did you know?"

"I can tell you have a good heart and enjoy being with other people and helping them, so I felt you must be a good teacher." She smiled in appreciation.

I could feel the Lord's love for her and His desire to help her, but I also sensed that she had been caught up in the things of the world for such a long time that she was having difficulty untangling herself from their sticky web.

I continued cautiously. "In your teaching, you have looked up to many who you felt were great teachers and have tried to learn from them and follow their examples, haven't you?"

"Of course."

"Do you believe God is a good teacher?"

"Certainly."

"Then think about this. In one sense you have come to this temple-school to be taught by the Greatest Teacher of all—the Lord Himself. He knows everything, including how best to teach others the truths of eternity."

She was definitely paying attention, so I proceeded. "What would you think of a teacher who taught that 2 + 2 = 5?"

"That is ridiculous. No one would teach that."

"Yes, but what if someone did, and what if the students and their parents and even the school officials said that was fine because maybe 2 + 2 could equal 5?"

"That is silly."

"I know it is, but what if that were the case?"

"Well, the teacher should just stand firm and say that she was going to teach the truth, which is that 2 + 2 = 4."

"But what if the principal told that teacher that unless she started teaching that 2 + 2 could equal 5 she would get fired?"

"That is absurd. Truth doesn't depend on someone's opinion. It is true because it is true and—" She stopped mid-sentence. Her eyes lit up, and she exclaimed, "Oh, I see what you are saying. God is teaching us the truth in the temple and doesn't care what the popular opinions or trends of the day may be. He just sticks with the truth." She paused for a moment and then said, "I know I should believe what God says, but some of what I heard today is so different from what I have been hearing and thinking for years that I'm not sure I can believe."

"I know you can because I know you have a good heart and love God, and deep within yourself you know He loves you. Some things may seem difficult to understand right now, but remember—only truth lasts forever. In eternity, popular opinion, philosophies of men, or anything that is in conflict with eternal truth will fade away and cease to exist. In God's temple-school you are taught only eternal, unending truths—and that by the Greatest Teacher of all."

"So what you are saying is that I have to decide whether I trust God or not."

"That's right."

She took a deep breath and then replied, "I'd like to, but I don't know if I can."

"With the Lord's help and the help of your bishop, Relief Society president, and others, you can and you will. Think about it. You came to this temple-school because you chose to. Inwardly you knew this is where you should be and this is what you should be learning. Satan is trying to sow seeds of doubt or magnify concerns to keep you away from God's school. He has nudged you off course before and will continue to try to keep you away from the source of eternal light and truth. He knows that when you learn and accept the truths of eternity, you won't believe his deceptions or follow him and his associates. Even though he will rant and rave, you need not fear, because God, truth, and light are always more powerful than evil, error, and darkness. I promise you that as you sincerely ask for God's help, He will give it to you, and the forces of evil will not overcome you. Remember, however, that God has given you your agency, so you must decide."

She was silent for what seemed a long time. Then a smile began to creep across her face, and she finally exclaimed, "Wow! I'd never thought of it that way. Wow! Do I ever have a long way to go! I guess I'd better get started." She turned to her bishop and Relief Society president and said, "Can you just forget about what I said a while ago? I think I'd better keep coming and learning. I'll try to have a more open heart." You can imagine the smiles and tears that followed.

When they left my office, I knelt and thanked the Lord for His tender mercies, including this one. What a miracle! Through the Spirit of God, the woman's concerns had been alleviated, her heart was softened, and she had been blessed with willingness to return and humility to learn from the temple. And miraculously, all this despite hardly mentioning what her concerns were! Wherever anyone has a good heart, God finds a way to help that person.

I was still thinking of God's love and basking in the aura

of all those smiles and good feelings when I suddenly seemed to be conveyed to another setting. There, large crowds instantly became aware of important things that were happening. The heavenly headlines in this new setting were "Mary forgave Jane," "John repented," "Jim was baptized," and "Lisa went to the temple," each of which brought great happiness to the assembled crowds. As I sensed their joy, some verses of scripture went through my mind:

"There was joy in heaven when my servant Warren bowed to my scepter" (D&C 106:6).

"Your brethren in Zion begin to repent, and the angels rejoice over them" (D&C 90:34).

"You who have assembled yourselves together to receive his will concerning you: . . . the angels rejoice over you" (D&C 88:1–2).

"Ye are blessed, for the testimony which ye have borne is recorded in heaven for the angels to look upon; and they rejoice over you" (D&C 62:3).

The yelling and excitement surrounding world championships and other man-made victories last but a moment and then are quickly forgotten. But all gospel-centered achievements are known in heaven and bring rejoicing that lasts forever. Learning the truth, overcoming evil, and keeping temple covenants are what eternal life is all about.

As I reflected on this good sister's seeming dilemma, I could see clearly the huge contrast between the learning of the world and the learning of the temple. In the former, we may or may not be taught the truth. In the latter, we will always be taught the truth.

There are great scholars and wonderful teachers all over the world. Many of them humbly and effectively teach truth, but others do not. God gives us the gift of the Holy Ghost so we can discern what is true and what is not, and He expects us to seek truth wherever we can find it. Temple truths are a marvelous measuring rod by which we can measure everything else. What a blessing to go to the temple and be taught the pure truths of eternity, in the best way possible, by the Greatest Teacher of all.

Chapter 11

"MY TEMPLE"

I often invited small groups of temple workers to my office to visit and get better acquainted. I would ask them to tell me a little about their lives and how they had come to serve in the temple. I was always amazed at the variety of experiences and the interesting paths they had traveled to arrive at that point. In one group several individuals mentioned that they had lived for years in other places and had felt that the Salt Lake or Mesa or some other temple was "their temple." Since living in or around Idaho Falls and working in the Idaho Falls temple, however, they had come to feel that it was now "their temple."

For some reason their phrase "my temple" caused me to wonder why they or any of us might feel that way. The more I thought about it, the more questions I had. And the more I prayed about those questions, the more understanding I received. It is easy to use the words *my temple* or *my mission*, but to truly make something "mine" requires great effort, has deep meaning, and brings unfathomable blessings. It is not a small thing for God to speak of "My children" or "My Son" or for the Savior to speak of "My sheep" or "My blood"

or "My house" or "My kingdom" or "My Father's kingdom."
Here are some of the insights I gained.

God wants each of us individually to be able to call eternally important things "mine." We can do so by using the
opportunities and the "things" God gives us in the way He
asks us to. For example, when we serve a mission with all our
heart, mind, and soul, it becomes "my mission." Wherever we
sacrifice, teach, love, feel the joy of being accepted, the pain
of being rejected, and give our best efforts, our testimonies
are strengthened, and something important becomes "mine."
Even though all missions offer essentially the same opportunities, and all temples function basically the same, where
we serve with all of our heart becomes "my mission" or "my
temple."

There are many other gifts from God that we call
"mine," such as our bodies and our families. Everyone's body
comes from the same dust of the earth and will return to
that same dust. Nonetheless, "my body" is mine because it
is where God placed my spirit. It is where the true essence
of me lives—my personal temple. It is where I struggle and
grow, where I feel love and pain, where I experience life, and
where I learn. Families have many things in common such
as mother, father, daughter, son, etc. But my particular family
is mine because it is the family to which I came and where
I learn to love, help, feel sorrow, experience joy, and develop
relationships.

The same principles apply to other "my's" such as "my
town," "my school," "my people," "my country," "my world,"
and even "my universe." There are many towns, schools,
peoples, countries, worlds, and universes, yet one is "mine"

because that is where God sent me to grow, learn, and become more like Him.

All things of lasting value belong to God and are given to us to help us along the path back to Him. Only as we understand this truth and see everything through the eyes of eternity can we properly use anything, including the physical things of this earth. Thus, when we speak of "my car" or "my home" or "my money," we should see them as belonging to God and "belonging" to us only as His stewards. He wants us to use them to help ourselves and others live better, learn more truth, and be more effective in assisting Him "to bring to pass the immortality and eternal life of man" (Moses 1:39).

The Lord is very clear about this: "Behold, all these properties are mine, or else your faith is vain, and ye are found hypocrites, and the covenants which ye have made unto me are broken; and if the properties are mine, then ye are stewards; otherwise ye are no stewards. But verily I say unto you, I have appointed unto you to be stewards over mine house, even stewards indeed" (D&C 104:55–57).

As these thoughts circulated in my mind, my understanding expanded, allowing me to grasp at least a partial appreciation of such scriptural declarations as "Worlds without number have I created" or "As one earth shall pass away, and the heavens thereof, even so shall another come; and there is no end to my works" (Moses 1:33, 38) and "all of these [earthly trials] shall give thee experience, and shall be for thy good" (D&C 122:7).

It was humbling to realize that whenever I had special experiences or insights such as these, there were thousands, millions, even an innumerable host of others throughout the universe who have already had, or are now having, or will yet have this same type of learning experience. I could see how Christ is "in all and through all things, the light of truth" (D&C 88:6). What a joy to know that He personally cares about me and you and everyone else and has custom fit the exact circumstances that will provide the maximum growth and development of each of us.

Our spirit is really "us." When it taps into the power of God's Spirit, it gives us the ability to control "our" body and allows us to understand things we could not otherwise understand and to accomplish things we could not otherwise accomplish. Disciplining our spirit to control our physical body is the key to moving forward, outward, and upward in learning to control things that are beyond "us." If we (our spirit) can't learn to control our own body, which is "right here," how can we expect to control other things that are farther away?

By definition, our body and our spirit, when fully united, constitute our soul (see D&C 88:15; Alma 40:23). God's love fills the entire universe, so when we unite our soul with the truths of eternity as given in the temple, we move into the embrace of that love. It is my conviction that when we have fully embraced that love, it will not matter where we are in space or eternity, for wherever we are, we can be guided through unimaginable spaces at unthinkable speeds. We will be able to hear and feel and respond to the needs of others from everywhere as well as receive help from others from anywhere.

Just as the eternal value of our individual "temple body" comes from the divinely begotten spirit placed within it, so the eternal value and power of the temple derives from the divine power that resides therein. Thus, when a worthy individual (one whose earthly temple is properly disciplined)

Courtesy NASA, ESA, and the Hubble Heritage Team.

enters the house of the Lord (the temple of God) to worship the Lord and participate in sacred ordinances, that individual is transported to celestial realms by the things he is taught. As we learn and use this celestial communication system, we understand that our ancestors hold certain keys needed for our progression and we hold certain keys needed for theirs; together we become united in God's love, as part of His never-ending circle of truth. Of course, we always retain our individual identity and remain "ourselves" but choose to become "one" with the Infinite and thus participate more fully in the "great and marvelous . . . works of the Lord . . . which surpass all understanding in glory, and in might, and in dominion" (D&C 76:114).

As these principles became more clear to me, I understood that *my*, as in "my temple" or "my mission" or "my body," etc., becomes truly "mine" only as I integrate myself and my stewardship into God's eternal truths as revealed in the temple. It is in the temple that we receive the understanding and the endowment of power from God to achieve this integration.

The temple is also key to helping us learn how to achieve the most important *my's* of all—to know that God is "my Father" and that Jesus is "my Savior." Following His resurrection, Jesus told Mary in the garden: "Go to my brethren, and say unto them, I ascend unto *my* Father, and *your* Father; and to *my* God, and *your* God" (John 20:17; emphasis added).

Jesus has many titles, such as Lord, Savior, Redeemer, Prince of Peace, and so forth. He has not only allowed us the sacred privilege of coming to know Him as "my Lord," "my Savior," and "my Redeemer" but has also revealed that truly knowing Him is the key to obtaining eternal life (see John 17:3). The temple is the repository of knowledge that allows us to truly know Him.

I have learned from sacred personal experience that Jesus is "my Friend." He yielded His body, His comfort, His will, His all, to His Father and is one with Him. He will help us in every needed way both now and throughout eternity. I understand what Nephi meant when he said, "I glory in *my Jesus*" (2 Nephi 33:6; emphasis added). When each of us truly knows Him as "my Friend," we need not fear anything, for He is with us. Remember Paul's powerful testimony: "I can do all things through Christ which strengtheneth me" (Philippians 4:13; see also Alma 26:12).

Earlier in the day I had heard several workers use the phrase "my temple," and I saw a glow about them and wanted to understand what it meant. Throughout the day I asked for and received many answers. It was clear that these workers had become "one" with the Lord and His temple to such a degree that the glow of temple truths shone through them. The temple had become "theirs" just as it can become "ours." When this mortal life is over, what is "ours" will not be our wealth or fame but our relationship to God and to others, including our spouse, our family, our temple, our body, and other "ours," all of which have become ours through faith on Jesus Christ and obedience to Him and and full participation in His temple. What a blessing the temple is in helping us make eternally important things "mine."

This is my testimony: I know that Jesus is our Lord, our Savior, our Redeemer. I know He is "in all and through all things" (D&C 88:6), which includes all the eternal "my's" we can think of. Above all, I know Jesus is my Friend and your Friend and that everyone can know this for himself or herself. That precious knowledge is expressed in this tender line from a favorite hymn: "Oh, sweet the joy this sentence gives: 'I know that *my Redeemer* lives!'"[1]

Chapter 12

FULLY IMMERSED

When I was called on a mission in 1954, there was no Missionary Training Center, so I was sent directly to the mission field and told to learn the language and culture the best I could. When I finally arrived in Tonga, my first assignment was to a small island far from headquarters, inhabited by about seven hundred people, none of whom spoke English. Of necessity I became fully immersed in the language and learned it much as a child does. I made lots of mistakes and was laughed at many times, but with the help of the scriptures, the Spirit of the Lord, and many hospitable people, I eventually learned to understand and speak the Tongan language and adapt to the unfamiliar culture. It took a little longer that way, but it really *took*. Even now, nearly sixty years later, I am still as comfortable speaking Tongan as I am speaking English and consider both to be my *native* tongues. Much of what we learn from full immersion stays with us and becomes part of us.

Since the Lord understands the lasting power of full immersion, He asks us to serve Him with *all* our "heart, might, mind and strength" (D&C 4:2). He gives us unlimited opportunities to become fully immersed in many good things, such as missions, parenting, temple work, callings in the Church, etc. In fact, our time on earth could be seen as one giant immersion experience. We experience great joy when we are fully immersed in building the kingdom of God in any way and want to help others experience that same joy (see 1 Nephi 8:12).

One special evening, I experienced firsthand the amazing joy and wonder that come from being fully immersed in temple work. Here is how it happened. Sister Groberg and I were often invited to speak at stake conferences or other meetings, where we always bore our testimony of the blessings of regular, voluntary, temple attendance. We testified to the stake presidents, bishops, and members that the temple was for them and promised them that by immersing themselves in it, they would receive corresponding joy. We tried to help them understand that our duty as a temple presidency was to see that everything in the temple was done properly, but their duty as leaders was to encourage the members to use the temple more fully and receive its blessings.

Many leaders and members knew of the great blessings that come from being immersed in temple work. They had experienced the vital role the temple plays in building strong testimonies and families and wanted to help others attend more regularly. There were still many, however, who had not yet experienced the blessings of full immersion in temple work. Long-standing traditions and practices, such as "once-a-month temple attendance" or the mistaken notion that "it is the responsibility of the high priests to do family history and temple work," were hard to overcome. Nevertheless, with patience, persistence, and the Lord's help, new and better attitudes began to prevail.

We occasionally had some sparsely attended sessions, and when we did, I felt I had failed to adequately explain and testify of the blessings of regular temple attendance. As I prayed fervently to know what more I could do, I received a reminder from the Lord that this was His work. My duty was to do my best and leave the rest to Him. I tried to have more faith, to be more humble and teachable, and testify with more sincerity, but I still became discouraged at times.

Then one day something special happened. I arrived at the temple, checked my schedule, and dived into my duties. I had an abundance of interviews for new ordinance workers. I was pleased that each one seemed committed and anxious to serve. Most of the sessions were quite full, and as the day progressed, they became even more so. By early evening, every session was filled to capacity, and some patrons had to wait for the next session or give service in some other area.

Despite the increasing number of patrons, everything ran smoothly. The shift coordinators were magnificent in their ability to perceive what needed to be done and then do it. They started extra sessions, provided the patrons with alternative opportunities to serve, and saw that everyone who came was immersed in temple service. Seeing the need, several sealers and ordinance workers volunteered to stay longer. The joy of being busily engaged in a good cause, or fully immersed, grew and grew. Miraculously, every soul who came to the temple that evening was accommodated in some meaningful way.

As the spirit of goodness and cooperation flowed through the temple, I received an impression, almost a command:

"Look!" So I looked. I saw the foyer filled with throngs of reverent patrons and workers radiating joy and fulfillment. I moved from room to room and saw that *every* room was filled to capacity with happy people who, like angels, were anxiously engaged in serving others.

This desire to help, along with gratitude for help received, merged into one great wave of goodness that softly rolled through the temple. It filled every inch of space and shone from every face. I felt as though I were floating in an element of light and love and warmth and glory, which included both "here" and "there" and was far beyond my ability to express. I remained enveloped in this ethereal feeling of goodness as my duties took me into several areas of the temple.

I went to the baptistry and looked. There I saw the whole area filled with young people and their leaders, glowing with goodness and a desire to serve. When I stepped into the font area, I breathed in warmth and purity as though I were breathing in the very essence of eternal life. Even though I wanted to stay, I knew there were other places I should go. Just as I turned to leave, I heard one of the witnesses quietly whisper to the baptizer, "You will need to do that one over—her foot came slightly out of the water. She needs to be *fully immersed* before you can proceed." They followed the established protocol, performed the baptism again, and proceeded on.

I returned upstairs with those words, *fully immersed before you can proceed,* reverberating in my mind. What a small thing—one foot slightly above the water for a brief moment—yet the witness said it must be done over. Only when she had been fully immersed could they move on. The truth of that principle made a deep impression on me. It is

Courtesy Intellectual Reserve, Inc.

when we fully accept the Savior with *all* of our hearts that we make true progress.

I remembered that Jesus was not only fully immersed by John in the River Jordan but stayed fully immersed throughout His life in loving and helping everyone. He left no one out. Not even the smallest "toe" was left out. He fulfilled everything and included everyone in His infinite atonement, His universal resurrection, and His full embrace of love and mercy. What an example of full immersion!

In our individual baptisms, it is only when we are fully immersed in water by proper authority that our baptism is valid and only when we are fully immersed in the spirit of love and helpfulness that we can be fully purified as by fire.

I thought about the consistent encouragement of angels and other witnesses whispering, "Immerse yourself fully, even if but for a moment. The joy you feel will give you increased desire to be immersed more fully, more often and in more ways."

The rest of the evening I continued to move from room to room and area to area and did all I could to encourage, help, and thank the wonderful workers and patrons for their service. All too soon the last session ended, the final patrons and workers left, and the evening cleaning process began.

I went to my office still floating in that supernal element of goodness, filled with wonder and amazement at all that had happened. While thanking God for this outpouring of celestial light and understanding, I began to have even deeper feelings about these eternally important principles. I became more aware than ever of what a truly sacred place the temple is. There are things about the temple of which we should not speak, but there are things about the temple of which we should speak—we should speak about that which the scriptures and modern prophets have said. When they say the temple is a bit of heaven on earth, that is not just a nice phrase. It is a statement of truth that can be comprehended by all who fully desire to know.

My mind filled with thoughts of the Millennium. It became clear that while we may need to wait for that specific period of time to enjoy its fulness, we do not need to wait till then to experience its warmth and love and goodness. We can become totally immersed in light and goodness and feel God's love for everyone on both sides of the veil, right here, right now. I know because I have felt it! When we become totally immersed in God's work of blessing and helping others, especially in the temple, we become tethered to the truths of eternity that allow us to hear and feel unspeakably beautiful things, things that cleanse and purify and magnify.

It became very clear why Satan and his minions do all they can to keep us from the temple. They know that the temple is full of light and truth, and they cannot operate in light and truth, only in darkness and deception. Light always banishes darkness. Truth always overcomes falsehood. God, who is Light and Truth, is always more powerful than Satan. Going to the temple and immersing ourselves in the light and truth found there allows God to give us greater strength to overcome the wiles of Satan. The greater the immersion, the greater the power to overcome. Eventually, through the Savior, the adversary will be completely overcome.

Our temple was not filled to capacity all the time, but it was much of the time. Likewise, we may not be *fully immersed* all of the time, but we can be for periods of time. During those times of full immersion—be it an hour, an evening, or only a brief moment—we can become so filled with joy and love that we become changed individuals. With faith and effort and help from above, we can repeat this immersion again and again and again, until we arrive at the "perfect day," as God has affirmed: "That which is of God is light; and he that receiveth light, and continueth in God, receiveth more light; and that light groweth brighter and brighter until the perfect day" (D&C 50:24). There is no better place to start this process than in the temple. If we would spend a day there, or a half-day, or enough time to do two sessions in a row, we would feel more immersion.

When we become fully immersed in God's work, for any period of time or in any area, be it missionary work, temple work, or something else, He blesses us beyond compare. As those times of full immersion become longer and more frequent, they define who we are. I know that being fully immersed in light and love is being at home with God.

I am realistic enough to understand that maybe not every person in the temple that evening was *fully immersed,* but I am also idealistic enough to believe that, as a whole, they were. The Lord blessed them individually and collectively, and they became *fully immersed* for that time.

I thought of the city of Enoch and wondered if everyone there was of equal worthiness or immersion. Maybe not, but all were of sufficient worthiness and were immersed enough to be part of that great transition. They were in the right place, at the right time, doing the right thing. Similarly, maybe not everyone in the temple that evening was of equal worthiness, or immersion, but they were all of sufficient worthiness and immersion to be in the right place, at the right time, doing the right thing. Maybe not everyone in Enoch's city or in the temple were fully immersed to begin with, but the effect of those who were fully immersed and those who were worthy enough to be there was powerful enough to draw everyone into that eternally expanding orbit of complete immersion.

As I pondered these truths, another thought came to my mind. The temple doesn't need to be completely full for there to be full immersion, though during the Millennium it may be. At any given time there are individuals in the temple, in homes, on missions, or elsewhere, who are fully immersed in God's work. No one could be more fully immersed in God's work than the Savior was in Gethsemane. Even though He was basically alone, He was fully immersed and not distracted by anything.

Courtesy Intellectual Reserve, Inc.

Jesus Praying in Gethsemane, *by Harry Anderson.*

At times I have been immersed in a good cause but have allowed some distraction, some concern, some fear, similar to a toe slipping out of the water, to stop my progress for a while. Many of us may be that way. I am deeply grateful that the Savior understands us and continues to help us move forward. Even when we take a step backwards, He is there to help us achieve the full immersion needed to proceed forward.

Whenever we immerse ourselves in building God's kingdom in any way—in the temple, in the family, as a missionary, in doing home or visiting teaching, etc.—we receive an infusion of energy, light, and strength that cannot be explained in human terms but is nonetheless real and lasting. This full immersion takes on a life of its own and ultimately comes to full fruition, no matter how long it takes.

When I left the temple that evening, I noted that I had

been busily and happily engaged in the Lord's work for more than ten hours, yet I remained energized and felt as fresh as a daisy. I recommitted to never complain and always be grateful for the opportunity to be fully immersed for long hours or days or even a lifetime in the work of the Lord. After all, that is where the fulness of joy is—and that is the goal.

Chapter 13

COMING HOME

A middle-aged couple visited my office in the temple. With radiant faces they asked if they could talk with me for a moment. I invited them in, and the husband said, "Jane and I have been to three sessions today. After the last one we spent some time in the celestial room and had the feeling that if you were still here, we would like to tell you what wonderful workers you have. They have all been very kind and helpful to us." They looked at each other, and then with a bit of a catch in his voice and a little mist in her eyes, he proceeded, "We also want to tell you that after years of searching we finally feel that we have come home." After a brief hesitation he concluded, "That's all. Thanks for your time."

There was a special warmth and goodness about them, and I asked if they would give me a little more detail. They nodded and between them told me their story.

She had been reared in a less-active home not too far from Idaho Falls. He had grown up in a nonmember home in the Midwest. Religion had not been a very big part of either of their lives. At eighteen she left home for a job in

California, where she met him while he was serving in the military. They eventually married and had two sons. At one point they had wondered if a church might be helpful in raising their boys and discussed it a little, but since their chosen military career brought frequent transfers and a busy life, they hadn't done anything about it.

When their sons became teenagers, serious challenges presented themselves, and once again they discussed religion as a possible help. She mentioned that she had been reared a Mormon and knew the Church had good youth activities. He wasn't sure what church he might have been a member of, so they decided to try the Mormon Church.

They found some information about the Church on their base and began attending. But before long they were transferred again. When they arrived at their new base, they were surprised and happy to find that someone had sent word ahead, and a missionary couple met them.

After receiving teaching and fellowshipping, the four of them were baptized. Their oldest son soon left for college but unfortunately did not stay active in the Church. The parents and their younger son became quite active and were very happy. They were transferred a few more times and fortunately found good Church support wherever they landed.

They were very concerned for their oldest son, as he was beginning to live in dangerous ways and rebuffed their efforts to help him change course. Their youngest son, on the other hand, stayed true, and when he turned nineteen received a call to serve a mission. He was excited and invited his older brother to come to the sacrament meeting where he would be speaking before leaving. His brother half-heartedly responded that he would try to come.

Two weeks before the sacrament meeting, they received a call that their oldest son had been killed in an auto accident. They were devastated. Their world turned upside down. But their youngest son held to his desire to serve a mission. After the funeral, he assured his parents that things would be all right. He had been studying the missionary discussions and shared many important principles with his parents, including details of the plan of salvation. Despite their having been members of the Church for a few years, they had not yet been to the temple. Their missionary son asked them to come to the temple when he received his endowment, but they did not feel ready. He challenged them to be ready by the time he returned so they could go to the temple and be sealed as a family. They promised they would try.

Their son served a wonderful mission, and with the encouragement he included in his letters, the help of dedicated local leaders, and their desire to fulfill his request, his parents were ready for the temple when he returned. The whole family, including the deceased son, was sealed for eternity. Their missionary son remained active, attended college, married in the temple, and eventually took a job in southeastern Idaho.

When the couple received their next transfer, they decided to retire from the military at the end of that tour of duty and began thinking about where to live and what to do for the rest of their lives. Since the wife's roots were close to where their son now lived, they decided to move there and be close to him and his family.

For the first time in their married life, they now felt a sense of permanency. Their new ward and stake quickly got them involved, and month by month they increased in their understanding of the gospel. Even though they had not been back to the temple since their sealing some years earlier, their bishop asked them to help teach a temple preparation course. At first they declined, saying they didn't know enough, but eventually they accepted the assignment to team-teach with another, more experienced couple. The course lasted several weeks with four other couples attending.

As they prepared the lessons and helped teach each week, their testimonies and desire to be in the temple grew steadily stronger. Before long they had their recommends and were attending the temple regularly. The more they attended, the better they felt. Now, after spending most of the day in the temple, they were in my office telling me how much they appreciated the ordinance workers and how, after much wandering, they finally felt they were "home."

I explained that this feeling was from God, and because the temple actually is His home on earth, it whispers to their spirits that they have been in these familiar surroundings before. Holding each other's hand, they whispered, "Yes, we know." I sensed an even deeper radiance about them than before.

When they left, I pondered on their joy at "being home." I recalled a widower who had spoken to me not long before, saying that someone had told him he was too old to come to the temple as often as he did and suggested he stay home. "But, President," he said, "this *is* home. I *am* home in the temple. Everything is familiar—the softness, the whiteness, the kindness, the love, the forgiveness, the helpfulness, the mercy, the promises, the opportunities, the ordinances, the duties, the desire to be better—this is where I want to be."

I assured him he was welcome to come "home" anytime he could.

He passed away a few weeks after this conversation. I attended his funeral, and at one point I seemed to see him smiling and saying, "You see, it really is home."

I better understood the universal longing we all have to "go home" or to invite lost loved ones to "come home." Being in the temple transcends time and space, for planted deep within each of us is a desire to "be home" in a place where we feel safe, loved, and needed and are surrounded by family. Those feelings are actually echoes of what we felt in our heavenly home. That is why the world's great art, music, and literature are saturated with the theme of wanting to be "home." Regardless of language, culture, or era, the feelings generated by the theme of longing for and going home resonate in every heart. We are touched by masterfully crafted poems, such as Robert Louis Stevenson's "Requiem":

> Under the wide and starry sky
> Dig the grave and let me lie:
> Glad did I live and gladly die,
> And I laid me down with a will.
> This be the verse you grave for me:
> Here he lies where he longed to be;
> Home is the sailor, home from sea,
> And the hunter home from the hill.

Many have been moved by such flowing musical passages as Antonin Dvorak's hauntingly beautiful theme commonly called "Going Home." Many have felt inspired, even brought to tears, by songs involving home, such as a current favorite from the Broadway musical *Les Miserables* entitled "Bring

Him Home." Most of us have also been captivated by paintings of pastoral scenes with a simple title, such as *The Hills of Home*.

These feelings for home become even stronger when we read the scriptures, pray, listen to our leaders, and attend the temple. At these and other similar times, something stirs within us and recalls faintly remembered feelings and dimly perceived settings that we know are real.

In addition to placing within each of us this longing to "come home," the Lord has placed temples (His homes) on earth where we can go and fulfill that longing. When we go to the temple, we respond literally to his invitation to "come unto him" (Matthew 11:28). There are many ways to come to Him, but perhaps most fulfilling is to come to His temple. When such prophets as Moroni exhort us to "come unto Christ, and be perfected in Him" (Moroni 10:32), they are inviting us to come to His temple, for that is where He is and where He will perfect us. In the temple He will meet us and teach us the things we need to do to ultimately come home and live with Him forever.

The scriptures explain that during His earthly ministry, Jesus "taught daily in the temple" (Luke 19:47). I know He continues to do so in our day.

The words and melody of a beautiful hymn by Isaac Watts, "My Shepherd Will Supply My Need," flowed through my mind. As the last phrase came, "no more a stranger, nor a guest, but as a child at home," I saw again this special couple who after years of wandering had finally found their way home. How wonderful to know that whenever we want to go home and be with Jesus, we can go to the temple. He is there and will let us know that we have come home.

Chapter 14

OVERCOMING ANGER

I met Mary when she came for an interview to be a temple ordinance worker. She surprised me somewhat by saying, "You are God's representative in the temple, and I want His assurance through you that I am worthy of this sacred calling." She continued, "Before you proceed, I need to tell you of my journey to this moment." As we visited, I was impressed by her candor and humility and intrigued by her description of her journey to peace. We can all learn much from her story.

Mary was raised in the Church and had been active most of her early life. She went to college and, after a short acquaintance, married a returned missionary in the temple. For several years they had a happy life. They attended church meetings fairly regularly, occasionally went to the temple, and had three children.

Her husband, Ted, had a good job and moved up steadily in his company. Before long he was required to travel a lot and began to spend more and more time away from home. Their children had good friends and were happy, but Mary felt lonely and uneasy about going to church or the temple without Ted. Her uneasiness grew as she began to notice that even when Ted was home, he seldom went to church and never to the temple. He used such excuses as he was "too tired" or "had other things to do."

One day Ted came home and announced that he had found a woman in a distant city whom he declared was his true soul mate. He said he had decided to live with this other woman, and that was final. He gave Mary divorce papers to sign and told her that she and the children would be well taken care of. He promised to leave the house debt free and give her full custody of the children because his "soul mate" was "not much into children." As you might imagine, Mary was devastated.

The events of the next few weeks seemed like one giant blur to her as she met with attorneys, mechanically signed papers, and cried—all the while trying to make sense of what was happening to her and her forever family. The blow to her heart, mind, and spirit was so deep that as she said, she almost ceased to exist.

When Ted was gone for good, she became even more despondent, especially as she watched the children—ages fourteen, twelve, and nine—struggle with the upheaval in their lives. Despite the help of her family, bishop, Relief Society leaders, and others, the world she had known seemed to disintegrate right before her eyes. She questioned her worth, wondered where she had gone wrong, and tried to figure out what she had done or failed to do to cause this unimaginable situation.

Her friends did what they could to build her up; however, she continued to blame herself and slowly sank into a shell from which she did not want to leave. In a somewhat zombie-like manner she cooked meals, got the children off to school, and moved through her daily routine. In her depressed state, she found herself questioning almost everything, including the significance of the Church and religion. Fortunately her family and friends stayed close, and the ward gave her and the children good support. The children eagerly grasped this help, but Mary tended to shy away from it.

She prayed sporadically but increasingly found praying difficult and fruitless. Eventually she quit praying at all. She went to church "mostly for the children's sake," but when invited to go to the temple, she declined. Even though helpful and concerned people surrounded her, she felt empty and cold inside.

One day, while the children were at school, she sat down, looked around, and was bombarded with feelings of anger, resentment, and frustration. As her anger escalated, she began yelling. "This is all Ted's fault. I am the innocent victim. How could he do this and get away with it? It's not fair. I'll get even with him some way."

Those dark feelings raged, and before long she was so angry she started throwing things. She had calmed down some by the time the children came home, but they immediately sensed a difference and asked if she was all right. She said she was fine, even though she knew she wasn't.

Over the next few years her emotional state grew more unstable. The angrier she became, the more depressed she became. Her family, her home and visiting teachers, and others tried to help, but she remained in a dense fog. Fortunately, the children did well in school and remained active in the Church, largely due to the encouragement of good friends and leaders.

Eventually her oldest daughter left for college. Mary

accepted her daughter's departure in a resigned sort of way. A little later her son announced he was going to go on a mission. She knew she should be happy and excited for him, but because she had allowed chronic anger to take such a hold on her, she saw this as another abandonment and snapped, "What good did a mission do your father?" She immediately regretted saying it.

From the shocked look in her son's eyes and his hasty retreat to his bedroom, she knew she had wounded him deeply. She wanted to apologize and assure him of her love and support but found herself immobilized.

When she finally started toward his room, the evil one, clothed in robes of anger and resentment, jumped up and slammed into her "like a steaming river of molten lava." Amid the boiling and crackling heat, the thought came into her head: *Apologize for what? Your ex is at fault. He is the con artist. He left you. You are justified in how you feel and what you said.* She tried to push those thoughts away but found she had become so deeply entangled in the cords of anger, bitterness, and self-pity that she was having difficulty doing so.

Reaching for every reserve she could find, she marshaled enough strength to push her way to her son's bedroom. As she opened the door, she saw him kneeling by his bed. A sob escaped her trembling lips. He immediately jumped up and asked what she wanted. She was shaking badly but managed to whisper, "Please help me. Could you pray for me? Or could we even pray together?" She took courage in the softness that came to his eyes. He extended his hand, and they knelt in prayer. When he asked God to bless his mom, the power and love she felt in his words of faith were both thrilling and frightening. Thrilling in that she felt love and help

Pondering, *by Dan Burr.*

beckoning to her, frightening in that they seemed so far away she wasn't sure she could reach them. It was as though she were struggling to wake from a dark coma and reconnect to light and love.

When the prayer concluded, she tearfully thanked her son for his worthiness and his help and asked him to keep praying for her. She apologized for her outburst and expressed her love and support for him. He said he loved her too and promised to keep praying for her.

She wanted to reach the light and the love she had felt and wanted to be rid of the anger engulfing her but found it was very difficult. There were times when she almost gave up. Her friends, her family, and especially her son remained faithful, and eventually she "began coming out of the 'coma' and moving from the darkness and death of anger into the light and life of God and forgiveness."

She received great comfort and help from her missionary son's prayers and letters. By the time he returned from his mission, she was attending church and participating regularly.

Soon after his return, her oldest daughter became engaged to be married. By the time of the wedding, Mary was ready to return to the temple and began coming often. A few years later her son announced his upcoming marriage in the temple. About the same time her youngest daughter announced her engagement. After those temple marriages, Mary was without dependents and asked her bishop about the possibility of becoming a temple worker, which is what had brought her to my office.

In Mary's words: "For years I let my reaction (which I could control) to Ted's actions (which I could not control) take away my peace. I allowed it to slow and even stop my prayers and remove me emotionally from the very people and powers that loved me and could help me.

"Before I really understood the temple, I rationalized that those who said I should forgive Ted didn't understand my situation, because if they did they would know how justified my anger was. In the temple, I learned that the Savior understands everyone's situation, including mine. He has been through much worse and still forgives. He simply does not retain bad feelings toward those who hurt Him. Instead He shows love for them. He even laid down His life for them. I have not been hurt as much as He has.

"In the temple I learned that I could not make meaningful progress until I overcame unkind feelings towards everyone, including Ted. There was no shortcut. I had to do it. I couldn't justify Ted's actions, but I had to learn to leave judgment to Jesus. He alone paid the price for all of us. He alone understands everything. He alone will be the final judge. I learned to trust Him fully and let go of the anger and vindictiveness I had felt all those years.

"I learned that we must 'deny [our]selves of all ungodliness' (Moroni 10:32). I had wanted to deny myself of some ungodliness but still cling to some. Before the temple became a big part of my life, I would say, 'Look at all Ted did to me.' Now I say, 'Look at all Jesus does for me. Since He holds nothing back, neither should I. He suffered not only for me but for everyone, including Ted. Judgment is up to Him, not me.'

"I even learned to pray for Ted and hope that he might find repentance. It is hard to pray for those who despitefully use you, but with God's help it is possible. God is forgiving and wants us to be forgiving also.

"The more I went to the temple, the more I wanted to be rid of unkind feelings toward anyone. The Lord helped me, and though I am far from perfect, I can now honestly say I am free of unkind feelings! There are many reasons the Savior could be angry with me and my stubbornness, but He chose not to be. He showed me a better way. He showed me how to overcome anger and every other evil from my life so I could move toward Him and feel the peace and joy of eternal life that is in Him. His way is the only way. Anything that keeps us from Him keeps us from peace and leaves us in torment.

"President, I feel that the anger that was in my life for so long is gone, swallowed up and overcome in His goodness. Do you know what that means to me?

"I will always need God's help, for there is much in life that still arouses anger and bad feelings, but I know that He will continue to help me. I know what it is to be filled with anger and what it is like to be free from anger. I want to help others be free. I think I am ready to be a temple worker, but the real question is, as God's agent, do you?"

I looked into her eyes and could see shining there a soft glow of genuine humility and the reflection of an honest heart. I said to her, "You are ready. I will now set you apart."

As I set her apart and spoke the words "authorized worker in the Lord's house," I heard a tiny gasp and felt a slight trembling as though the power of God were purging the last vestiges of anger and self-pity from the soul of this faithful woman.

When I finished the blessing, she whispered, "Thank you. Thank you for the opportunity to serve here. I sincerely want to help others find the joy I have found." I knew these words were addressed to God and to all who had helped her get to that point. And I knew, as did she, that the setting apart was done with God's approval.

When Mary left, I felt as though an ethereal essence remained in the room, an aura that comes from being in the presence of true humility and purity. It was the same feeling I had experienced decades before when President David O. McKay visited with a few of us missionaries in Tonga. He gazed into each of our faces and encouraged us to love the Lord and love the Tongan people and be good missionaries. The love and purity and beauty that emanated from him were so overpowering that I have never forgotten them. That is always the way we feel in the presence of good, pure people, and how we will feel in the presence of God, who is the epitome of purity!

I closed the door and thanked God for Mary and for those who had helped her. I thanked Him for the temple, for

ordinance workers, for patrons, and for good people everywhere who with pure hearts earnestly strive to help others
in their efforts to overcome anger and every other form of
evil. I knew God would deal gently with Mary and with
everyone who "believeth that salvation was, and is, and is to
come, in and through the atoning blood of Christ, the Lord
Omnipotent" and who "yield[s] to the enticings of the Holy
Spirit, and putteth off the natural man and becometh a saint
through the atonement of Christ the Lord and becometh as
a child, submissive, meek, humble, patient, [and] full of love"
(Mosiah 3:18–19).

Truly it is godlike to be forgiving and gentle with one
another! I do not fully comprehend the scope of God's love,
grace, mercy, and forgiveness, but as I observed the beauty
and purity of Mary's spirit and remembered other similar experiences, I caught a glimpse of what might happen when we
truly repent and rely on the Savior. He promises not only to
forgive but to "remember [those sins] no more" (D&C 58:42;
see also v. 43; 64:9–11).

The Lord knows everything, so if He chooses to forget
something, I suspect that that "thing" doesn't exist anymore.
There are many things I, and I believe all of us, would like
God to forget. I believe Him when He says He will, if we
truly repent. I wondered if in some marvelous, presently incomprehensible way this might be the key to how the universe might be cleansed from distraction and evil—simply
causing those things to cease to exist. As near as I could tell,
Mary's former anger did not exist anymore—a true miracle!

As I once more thanked God for helping Mary, and all of
us, overcome the anger that comes from feelings of betrayal,
it came to me that the ultimate betrayal is turning from God

and His Son after all they have done for us. God does not get angry at us for such betrayal but asks us to repent and change course so we won't suffer the misery that comes from such un-repented-of betrayal (see D&C 19:16–17).

How grateful I am for repentance, forgiveness, and new beginnings! How grateful I am for the temple with its power to help us overcome anger, complacency, worldliness, short-sightedness, selfishness, and every other weakness and impurity that would keep us from experiencing eternal joy. God loves and forgives and wants us to do likewise.

Chapter 15

MIRACLES AND MYSTERIES

Quite often a certain bishop came to the temple with his ward members for a chapel meeting and endowment session. One evening he asked if we could visit for a moment. He wanted to know the various possibilities and requirements for members of his ward to become ordinance workers or to serve in other ways in the temple.

I described the various opportunities and asked what motivated his query. He replied, "You came to our stake conference some time ago and promised us that if we made the temple a bigger part of our lives, we would receive more blessings. You said that in your opinion going to the temple once a month may have been fine a few generations ago, but with the increased presence and sophistication of evil and temptations in our day, we need extra fortification and should seriously consider attending the temple every week if our circumstances allow."

He went on, "When I heard that, I gulped and reasoned that with my busy schedule there was no way I could do that. However, something stirred within me, and I thought to myself, *Well, at least I could try.* At that very moment I felt a nudge and a smile from my wife. After conference we decided to do whatever we could to make the temple a bigger part of our lives.

"I had been serving as bishop for about two years and felt I had dealt with about every challenge possible. I was wrong. New ones kept coming. With all the interviews, interventions, activities, meetings, funerals, etc., I couldn't see how we could get to the temple more often, but we said we would try, so we did.

"I started delegating more, combining some meetings, and trying to make more efficient use of time. Before long I found myself in the temple nearly every week. I cannot explain what happened or how it happened, but six months later at our next stake conference, I realized that despite my spending extra time in the temple, everything was going better—in my family, my work, and my ward. Since this increased temple activity was helping me and my wife so much, I was sure it would do the same for my ward members.

"Over the next six months I did a lot of encouraging and by the time our next stake conference came, many ward members were attending the temple more regularly. I was careful not to assign or keep track but only encourage and tell of my experience and let each individual or couple do what they could. The members who made the temple a bigger part of their lives experienced the same blessings we did, so they encouraged their friends to do the same.

"I have now served as bishop for four years. During the first two, I was buried in challenges; the next one was still filled with challenges but seemed to go better; this last year has gone even better. I know it is because of the increased temple activity of the members. Many miracles have oc-curred in our ward. Let me tell you just one.

"Brother and Sister Smith both worked for the school district. When Sister Smith retired, she became an ordi-nance worker and hoped that when her husband retired, he would do the same. When he did retire, however, he told her he had worked long enough and had missed so much fishing and hunting that he was now going to make up for lost time.

"At about this time, one of their older daughters returned home to live with them. She noticed how happy her mother was from working in the temple, so she also became a temple worker. They hoped and prayed that their husband and fa-ther would join them some day. He supported them in their callings but continued to hunt and fish and do the things he felt he had 'earned the right to do.'

"One Sunday after dinner, they gathered the dishes to the kitchen, and the father announced that while the girls finished the dishes he was going to the living room to read the newspaper. Even though he loved his wife and daughter and knew of their goodness and of their desire for him to become a temple worker, he stubbornly said he was going to continue his hunting and fishing.

"He sat down, picked up the paper, and began to read. A feeling of calm came over him that he could only describe as a miracle. He had left the kitchen wanting to read the paper and not even think about becoming a temple worker. Now suddenly, he had lost all interest in the paper and was sure he should become a temple worker. He stood up, returned to the kitchen, and said, 'When I left a few moments ago, I didn't want to be a temple ordinance worker. Now, that is all I want to be. What do I need to do to make that happen?' You can imagine the joy and tears that followed.

"There have been many similar experiences in our ward since the members have been making the temple a bigger part of their lives.

"We still have a full complement of challenges, including people out of work, funerals, concerns with our youth, and other challenges, but somehow, everything is better. How does that happen?"

I said I didn't know for sure, but I did know that the Lord always keeps His promises. Since His prophet has promised that everyone who worthily enters the temple will come out a better person, that is what happens.[1] Those who voluntarily go to the temple more often become better people, so everything else about their life becomes better also.

I explained that while I didn't know exactly how it happens, I did know that it does happen. I quoted the Savior's words from the Bible where He said, "The wind bloweth where it listeth, and thou hearest the sound thereof, but canst not tell whence it cometh, and whither it goeth: so is everyone who is born of the Spirit" (John 3:8). I added, "So is every one that goes to the temple more frequently with a desire to serve. We don't know where these miracles come from, but just like the wind blowing from heaven, they do come."

The bishop nodded in agreement. It was obvious that he had great love and concern for his people and sincerely desired each of them to receive more blessings. He also understood that the temple is one of the best places for that to happen. As I watched him, I could almost imagine watching the Savior express His love for His people by encouraging them to come to His temple and receive the great blessings He has waiting for them there.

The scriptures tell us that in those days "all the people came early in the morning to him in the temple, for to hear him" (Luke 21:38). We have the same opportunity today. I hope we go to the temple "for to hear him" regularly.

We don't understand very much about the mechanics of the earth's orbit, or the sun, or our place in the universe, but we know God understands. We know He loves us and that the net effect of everything He does and asks us to do is to benefit us. Even though we sometimes call these things "mysteries," they are mysteries only to us, not to God! Whenever we put our whole heart into anything God asks us to do, we receive great blessings now, over time, and throughout all eternity.

Every day in every temple (and in worthy homes and other places) throughout the world and beyond, wherever anyone obeys God with full purpose of heart, miracles occur. Hearts are changed, love is strengthened, light is increased, and life is made more meaningful. Alma told his son, "Now, I unfold unto you a mystery; nevertheless, there are many mysteries which are kept, that no one knoweth them save God himself" (Alma 40:3). We don't need to know *how* they happen in order to know that they *do* happen (see Alma 26:22).

God's miracles and mysteries are actually manifestations of His love expressed in ways that, as yet, we do not fully understand. In His own time and way, we will eventually comprehend all these things and be even more grateful for what we now do not fully comprehend.

Chapter 16

"I TOLD YOU SO"

A couple came to my office, and the husband said, "I want you to be a witness as I apologize to my wife and to the Lord for my stubbornness of heart. My wife has attended the temple regularly for years; I have not. When our youngest son left home, she became an ordinance worker; I did not. For many years she has spoken of the beauties and blessings of the temple and encouraged me to come with her, but I would not.

"Time after time I dropped her off at the temple while I did something I felt was 'more important.' When I picked her up, she smiled, thanked me for taking her, and expressed her feelings of love and joy. When she asked how my evening had gone, I usually mumbled something like 'fine' or 'okay.' It irked me that she was so much happier than I was. I was hurting, but I could not bring myself to admit that she was right. I thought to myself, *It's not fair that you are happy and I am frustrated.* She never used the words, but I felt she was inwardly saying, 'I told you so.' I was angry at the thought that she was probably right. Who likes an 'I told you so'?

"I was raised in the Church, and we were married in the

temple, I pay tithing and attend most meetings, but somehow I convinced myself that I was too busy to attend the temple. It took a long time, but I finally humbled myself enough to ask my wife if we could go to the temple together. She simply said, 'That would be wonderful.' I told her I was a little afraid because it had been so long, but she assured me that the ordinance workers would help me.

"At first I felt awkward, but little by little, I began to feel at ease and at home. Recently I was set apart as an ordinance worker by one of your counselors. I truly enjoy this work!

"I now see how foolish I was to let pride and worldliness stand in my way for so long. I want you and all of the workers to know how much I love my wife, the Lord, and the temple. No one could be happier." He turned to his wife and said, "Thanks for being so patient with me." The glow of her face caused her tears to glisten and sparkle.

He shook my hand and said, "Thanks for listening and being a witness." They left my office, and as I watched them move down the hall, I marveled at how kind and patient the Lord is with us and what great blessings He gives us when we humble ourselves and go to the temple regularly.

I thought about this man's fear of the phrase "I told you so" and realized that most of us react the same way. Most of us don't like to be reminded of our shortcomings. When we eat foolishly and gain weight or do dumb things and get hurt or sick, we don't want our friends or our conscience to say, "I told you so." We may even harbor resentment toward those who do better than we do and secretly wish they would do more things wrong to help justify our own weaknesses.

The more I thought about this, the more I realized that the Lord always "tells us so" by explaining exactly what will happen if we keep His commandments or choose not to keep them. History and experience prove that He is always right, yet we still tend to shy away from believing Him and His prophets. I wondered why. I suppose part of it is that Satan, the great deceiver, keeps pointing out the inconsistency of mortal man and tries to convince us we can't trust anyone.

A mother once told me of a rule they had that each family member must wash his or her hands before eating. One young son constantly came to the table with dirty hands and was sent away each time to wash them. Finally in frustration the mother said, "Son, you know we always make you wash your hands before we eat, so why do you keep coming with dirty hands?" The little boy looked up and with an impish grin said, "One time you didn't." Consistency among men is hard to find. Consistency with God is always there.

If we found someone who was consistently right in temporal things, wouldn't we listen to him and do what he said? For example, if we found someone whose every stock recommendation was right, wouldn't we follow him and become rich? We don't find that consistency among humans, but we do with God. He and those who speak for Him are always right, and we can trust them all of the time. When they say, "If you do this—that will happen." Both positive and negative, it always happens. When ancient Israel, the Nephites, or others rebelled and followed a path contrary to God's commandments, they always reaped the dark consequences, which He had warned them would come. On the other hand, when the people kept His commandments, they always received the promised blessings.

Obeying the simple things He asks us to do, such as fasting, praying, paying tithing, practicing family unity, attending the temple, etc., brings us joy, and when we feel this joy we can almost hear Him say, "I told you so." When we perform our duties, serve others, keep our covenants, serve missions, or do anything He asks us to do, we experience joy and hear in our hearts His confirming words, "I told you so." When we overcome obstacles, such as enduring pain and suffering or forgiving and loving with all our hearts, the eventual reward is *always* glorious, just as He said it would be.

When the Savior was preparing to leave His disciples physically, He said, "In my Father's house are many mansions: if it were not so, I would have told you. I go to prepare a place for you" (John 14:2). He always tells us in advance, both good and bad, and He is always right.

At times I have imagined the smile on the Savior's face when He will show the faithful the magnificent mansions prepared for them and says, "I told you so." The Prophet Joseph Smith once saw in vision the place where God and Christ dwell and said of what he had been shown, "Great and marvelous are the works of the Lord, and the mysteries of his kingdom which he showed unto us, which surpass all understanding in glory, and in might, and in dominion" (D&C 76:114). Think of the promises made in the temple to those who are faithful. Could anything be more clear or more glorious? These promised blessings, which are dependent on our faithfully keeping our covenants, deserve our best efforts. The Savior characterized those blessings as being given in "good measure, pressed down, and shaken together, and running over" (Luke 6:38). What generosity.

As we go through life's ups and downs, we can depend on the Savior's promises. He continually encourages us: Don't faint. Keep going—keep believing—endure faithfully. You can make it. It is worth it. I will help you. I always keep my promises. What a blessing to hear from Him the comforting words, "I told you so," during our journey as well as at the conclusion of it.

I thought of this wonderful wife and realized that her actions more than her words had helped the Lord bring about a mighty change first in her heart and then in her husband's. She was faithful and patient for a long time and received a happy outcome. Then I thought of many others who have been just as faithful, just as desirous, just as patient with wayward husbands or wives, or children, or brothers, or sisters, but have not yet experienced that same happy outcome.

As I pondered these seeming contradictions, it was as though I heard a soft whisper saying, "In my own time and way every promised blessing will be received by the faithful. Man measures things in time; I measure things in faithfulness. I am faithful and consistent. When everything is right and every knee has bowed and every tongue confessed, every person will smile when I say, 'I told you so.'"

Chapter 17

BECAUSE IT IS RIGHT

One evening a sister who seemed very excited about something asked if she could talk to me for a moment. Her whole face seemed like one giant smile, and I wondered if she could even speak. After a deep breath she began, "I don't know where to start. I am so happy that I just had to share my joy of the temple with you. President, do you know how wonderful the temple is? You probably do, but I wonder how many people really do? I didn't until just a few months ago. In fact, tonight is the first time I have been so overwhelmed by the beauty and power of the temple that I am literally filled with joy. Can I tell you how this happened?"

I nodded, and she continued.

"I have been a member all my life. Bill and I were married in the Salt Lake Temple many years ago. Right after we were married, he took a job in the South, and we lived far from a temple. We went to church and considered ourselves active. However, looking back, I wonder if my activity was sort of on a grade-school level.

"We lived in the South for more than twenty years, had five children, moved a few times, went through the normal health, school, and job challenges but ended up with a nice home and a secure job. I hoped we would never need to move again. We all went to church and had good friends but seldom attended the temple because it was so far away.

"After twenty comfortable years, Bill informed me that the company he worked for was having financial problems and needed to downsize, which would probably include some lay-offs. We really worried about this and prayed for the best. Our older children were in college, and we decided not to tell the younger ones yet.

"A few days later Bill came home from work and said, 'We need to talk.' I was afraid he had lost his job. However, he told me that because of his many years with the company, they had given him three options: (1) He could take early retirement with a decent severance package and try to find other work in the area. (2) He could take a lower paying job with the company and stay on until full retirement. (3) He could take a job at a newly opened office in Idaho and stay at his current salary level.

"I was so relieved that he hadn't been laid off that I immediately blurted out, 'Whatever you say is fine with me.' He coughed a little and replied, 'I've been thinking we should move to Idaho.'

"Even though I had said that whatever he decided was fine with me, I immediately began to have second thoughts. Bill asked that we pray about it. After the prayer he became more excited, and I became more hesitant.

"We had lived in the South for so long that I was afraid I could not adjust to the cold winters in Idaho. I tried to be supportive but secretly resisted the move and tried to find some way to stay where we were. When it was apparent that moving was inevitable, I resigned myself to the move but my heart was not in it.

"We made the move a little more than a year ago, and the shock of the change was greater than I had anticipated. I was unhappy and sank into self-pity with a constant long-ing for my old friends and familiar surroundings. Fortunately our children were happy, and my husband loved his work. Though I felt guilty, I continued to be only partly there.

"Our bishop announced that the ward was having a 'temple evening.' Bill was excited to go, but for some reason I resisted. At his urging I finally went with him but with a poor attitude. It was a 'nice' experience but not a 'great' one for me. A few weeks later Bill said the ward was going to the temple again and he'd like us to go. I reminded him that we had just gone. I asked how often he thought we should go. He said he wanted to go as often as possible.

"I don't know why I resisted, but I did. I knew going to-gether meant a lot to him, but I still asked him to go by him-self this time because I just didn't feel up to it right then. He was disappointed and asked me to think about it some more.

"For the next few days I felt miserable. Instead of think-ing about the temple, I thought about how much I missed my friends and surroundings in the South. When Friday came, I was so despondent I simply said I wasn't going. He asked me why, and I replied, 'I just don't feel like it.' I thought that would end the discussion, but he said, 'I would really like us to go together. I know this move is hard on you, but since we are close to a temple, I feel we should go more often. I know things will get better for you and all of us as we do.'

"I still said, 'I just don't feel like it.' He was sad, and I felt pretty crummy, but he ended up going by himself.

"A few weeks later we went through the same discussion again. I don't know why I continued to resist. In another few weeks when he asked me again, the same old 'I just don't feel like it' came out almost automatically. This time, however, he looked me square in the eye and said, 'You say you don't feel like going, but I am asking you to go anyway because it is the right thing to do.' He seemed so determined that the only thing I could say was, 'Well, if you really want me to go that badly, I guess I could.'

"We went a few other times but mostly because of his urging. As the months went by I began to feel a little more comfortable in our new ward and somewhat more 'at home' in the temple. We planned on coming together tonight, but yesterday he was called away on an emergency business trip. He said we could go again when he returned. I just smiled and sent him off.

"When he left I felt such a love for my husband and such a desire to please him that I decided to come to the temple on my own. I knew that would make him happy. No sooner had I decided to do this than every concern I had ever had began to pound on me. 'You can't go alone. You've never done that before. Just stay home. You have lots of other things to do.' As these feelings assailed me, I remembered Bill's words: 'You say you don't feel like going, but I am asking you to go anyway because it is the right thing to do.'

"President, I did it! I'm here! I came on my own! Despite the feelings of inadequacy and fear I came anyway, just because it was the right thing to do. This is the first time in my whole life that I have ever come to the temple on my own. This evening has been so unbelievably wonderful that I had to tell someone about it. You can't imagine the joy I feel. I can hardly wait to tell Bill. He will be so happy.

"Of course, I want to come with my husband, but now I know that if circumstances arise where that is not possible, I can and will still come on my own. I hope I never resist again. I worry that many people still resist as I did because they don't know how wonderful the temple is, just as I didn't for a long time. Now I know how my husband feels. I want to help everyone feel that way! What can I do to help them feel this joy?"

I told her that as she radiates the joy she feels to those around her, they will soon catch the spirit of the temple. She smiled and said, "Thanks for listening. I just had to share my joy with someone. Isn't the temple wonderful?" An unmistakable glow followed her as she left.

I thanked the Lord for the temple, for this woman, for good husbands and wives and for faithful people everywhere who overcome fear or apathy and simply go anyway because it is the right thing to do. In my mind I could hear her husband patiently pleading with her to just go because it was the right thing to do and doing so would bring her great blessings.

Then I seemed to hear the Savior pleading with all of us to do the same—"Just go, so I can bless you!" The phrase "go anyway because it is right" filled my mind and brought forth many memories. I thought back to my freshman year at Brigham Young University. My sister and Jean's sister had become friends while playing in the violin section of the BYU Symphony Orchestra. They set up a blind date for Jean and me. I didn't want to go with someone I had never met, nor did Jean; however, we went anyway because we trusted our sisters. What blessings have come to us and our family from trusting good people and going anyway because it was the right thing to do!

I thought of the Savior asking if there were some other way and then saying to His Father, "Nevertheless not my will, but thine, be done" (Luke 22:42; see also Mark 14:36; Matthew 26:39). To me, in effect He was saying, "I trust Thee. I will go anyway because it is the right thing to do."

I was filled with wonder and gratitude for all that God has done and continues to do for each of us, even when it was hard and caused Him to "tremble because of pain, and to bleed at every pore" (D&C 19:18). I could see where a big part of all the good done in the world is done by those who, despite inconvenience, decide to do it anyway, because it is the right thing to do. I thought of fathers going to work even when they don't feel like it, of children doing chores when they would rather be doing something else, or mothers putting aside personal agendas and helping their children and others.

My mind filled with other "go anyway" experiences, most of which were positive with wonderful outcomes. I also remembered some times when I had not gone anyway but had allowed worldly concerns to persuade me not to go. As I remembered these occasions, I didn't feel condemnation so much as a loss of the things I might have learned or help I could have given had I gone anyway. I determined to do better next time. I also felt deep gratitude for my mission president, my parents, my wife, and many others, who have encouraged me to "go anyway because it is right," even when sometimes I didn't feel like it.

The Savior understands how we feel when we give in to fear or laziness or apathy and do not go anyway. He wants to free us from those guilty feelings and encourages us in every way possible to have more faith in Him and in His temple.

When we look back over our time in mortality, we will probably see obedience and growth much of the time, slippage and regression some of the time, but hopefully repentance and turning back to God all of the time. Only God can be the final judge of the events in our lives or the lives of others. Only He understands everything and applies the perfect balance of mercy and justice. We must leave judgment (even of ourselves) with Him and use all our energy to live so we can have His Spirit with us and receive the strength needed to do whatever He asks—because it is always right. As the Prophet Joseph Smith taught, "Whatever God requires is right, no matter what it is, although we may not see the reason thereof till long after the events transpire."[1]

When we trust God, not man or the world, listen more carefully to the sacrament prayers, and live more in tune with them, we will "always have his Spirit to be with [us]" (D&C 20:77), and we will go where we should go and do what we should do.

I felt love and gratitude for Bill, whom I had not met but who, I knew, was kind and persistent, similar to the way God is. I had equal gratitude for his wonderful wife, who, after listening to her husband's counsel in righteousness and to the Spirit of the Lord, had gone anyway because it was right and experienced such great joy.

All of life can be glorious when we listen to and obey the Spirit of the Lord—even when that Spirit includes the encouragement, *I know it is hard, and maybe you don't feel like it at times, but I want to bless you, so I ask you to just go anyway because it is right.*

Chapter 18

RESTORATION

When President Gordon B. Hinckley called me and Sister Groberg to serve as president and matron of the Idaho Falls Idaho Temple, he emphasized, among other things, his desire to keep the temple as close as possible to its "original design."

As soon as he said those words, a memory from my youth began to stir in my mind. Aren't memories fascinating? Some are pleasant, some are not; some stay with us, some are forgotten, and some remain dormant for years until awakened by a specific event, such as when President Hinckley spoke the words *original design*.

To explain this memory, come with me to the late 1930s when the original design of the Idaho Falls temple began. As a young boy, I watched the temple slowly rise on its location on the bank of the majestic Snake River. But World War II began before the temple was completed, and construction came to a crawl. During those war years I watched newsreels at our local movie theater showing death and destruction from the war. The scenes scared me. My father was serving as bishop, and I observed his sorrow when he went to comfort families

Courtesy, D. V. Groberg family photo collection.

Cornerstone-laying ceremony at Idaho Falls temple, October 1940.

who had lost sons or husbands in the war. I also witnessed his joy at the building of the temple. As the war progressed, I observed two things taking place—the walls of the temple rising higher and higher and the forces of freedom gradually prevailing over the forces of evil. These concurrent events made an indelible impression on me. Finally, in 1945 the war ended, and shortly thereafter the temple was completed.

I remember the blazing headlines, the honking horns, and the joyous outpourings of thanks for the ending of the war. I also remember the deep joy and reverent gratitude for the completion of the temple. I was sure there was a connection between the completion of the temple and the end of the war. To me each event represented the triumph of good over evil and life over death. I knew the world would be a better place because of the defeat of the Axis powers and the concurrent completion of the temple. My parents explained that the temple would help everyone, including those who had died during the war. That made me feel warm inside.

Servicemen and servicewomen began returning home, and soon dates were set for the open house and dedication of the temple. I wasn't old enough at age eleven to attend the dedication, but I was allowed to go to the open house. I was very excited to see the inside of the temple. My parents had talked so much about its power and beauty that I fully expected to see or feel something marvelous there, and I was not disappointed.

As we moved quietly from room to room, I was impressed with the peace and beauty of everything. When we entered the celestial room, however, I was awestruck by what I saw there. My eyes were drawn up, and up, and up. The ceiling rose in tiers, and the highest part in the center seemed to go right into the sky. I was sure it went all the way to heaven. The boyhood memory of that window to heaven was indelibly etched on my mind.

Shortly after the open house, Church President George Albert Smith and all the other General Authorities visited Idaho Falls for the temple dedication—just the eighth operating temple built in this dispensation. I listened with fascination as my parents and my older sisters talked about participating in the marvelous dedication. In my mind's eye I kept seeing the center of the temple going all the way to heaven.

As a boy, I often walked around the temple grounds, and when I turned twelve, I did baptisms in the temple. It was not until I received my mission call, however, that I again went through the entire temple. I was excited to receive my endowment and looked forward to being in the celestial room where I could again see all the way to heaven. Everything about my experience in the temple was wonderful, and when we entered the celestial room, it was beautiful and I felt good.

I was a little taken aback, however, when I saw that the windows were gone and the ceiling had been lowered, so I could no longer see all the way to heaven in the same way as before. I asked someone what had happened and was told that the original ceiling had been lowered in an effort to conserve heating costs. They understood that that was to be a temporary measure, but apparently people got used to it, forgot the original design, and never changed it back. My experience in the temple was so marvelous and I was so excited about going on a mission that I didn't think much more about the change in the configuration of the ceiling.

After my mission, Jean and I were married in the Los Angeles temple, and after finishing my schooling, we returned to Idaho Falls to live. I was called as a bishop, and we attended the temple often. I heard several people talk about the special feeling they had experienced during the original open house and even heard some talk about restoring the celestial room ceiling to its original design, but nothing happened. Years went by, and one by one those who had experienced that original 'upward pull' passed to the other side of the veil and most of the talk about that particular restoration passed with them.

A few years later I was called to be a General Authority and was asked to move near Church headquarters in Utah. Over the next thirty years, Jean and I lived in many parts of the world and attended many temples. Only rarely were we able to return to the Idaho Falls temple. Then thirty years after leaving Idaho Falls and sixty years after my open house experience, President Hinckley called me back to Idaho Falls to serve as the temple president and emphasized the words *original design*.

Being a temple president and matron was a new experience for Jean and me, and we had much to learn and do. No matter how busy we became, however, President Hinckley's words *original design* continued to ring in my heart and mind. Despite our busyness, the wonder and awe I had felt as a youth in seeing all the way to heaven would not leave me and in fact became stronger. I had the feeling that the Lord was saying, "The time for this restoration has come."

Eventually, our presidency submitted a recommendation to restore the celestial room to its original design. For a long time we heard nothing, but eventually, a dialogue on this restoration project began. At times it was encouraging and at other times discouraging. I guess I needed to be reminded of how much time and effort it takes to accomplish anything good and important.

The daily work of the temple kept me very busy, and the restoration project was often pushed to the back of my mind but never fully left my consciousness. From time to time there was a little movement here, a new question there, or another form to be filled out somewhere else, but overall, it was hard to see much progress. There seemed to be roadblocks everywhere, and I often found myself pleading with the Lord for patience and understanding. During some of the more discouraging times, I received the distinct impression that though I should keep working on the restoration, my main responsibility was to see that the temple work was being done properly and with love. I was admonished to remember that the temple was still *the temple* with all of its beauty and power, regardless of what might happen with this particular restoration project.

I tried to work harder, be more patient, and increase my

trust in God, but I must admit that at times I still became discouraged. After one major setback to this restoration project, I poured my heart out to the Lord and received a distinct impression that, in effect, said, *Leave this with Me. It is My house. I appreciate your concern and hard work, but I, not you or any other mortal, will bring it about when it is right. Your main concern is to just move forward with the eternally important work of the temple.*

What a blessing it was to have reaffirmed to my soul that God is all knowing, all powerful, and totally in charge of the whole universe, including His temple and this particular restoration project! He has a prophet in place, directs him aright, and always does what is best when it is best! As we do our best, we can leave the rest to God, including the timing. He can see and comprehend things we cannot. I relearned that when we put everything, including our lives, into His hands, He gives us a peace that truly goes beyond understanding.

I learned that real faith is when there are no more *if's* in our hearts. With His help, I got to the point where I knew this restoration *would* happen; I just didn't know *when* or *how*. I also realized that this restoration project was very small compared to things for which other people have put their very lives on the line.

For example, some of the believers in Book of Mormon times were threatened with death if the sign of the Savior's birth, in which they believed, did not occur by a certain time. These faithful followers of Christ remained at peace because the *if* of His coming was gone from their hearts. Only the *how* and the *when* remained to be determined.

Many Nephite prophets knew the record they were keeping of their experiences would come forth in the last days.

They perhaps didn't know that it would be called the Book of Mormon or exactly how it would be manifest, but they had no *if*'s about its coming forth, so they left the *how* and *when* to God as they continued to faithfully do whatever He asked them to do. Many ancient prophets and other faithful people likewise knew the Savior *would* come and that there would be a final restoration of the gospel in the last days. Because they had no *ifs*, they simply lived their lives faithfully and didn't worry about the *how* or *when*. I'm sure the same is true of the return of the Savior and the coming of the Millennium. Though we don't know exactly how it will all occur, our best course is to live the gospel as best we can and leave the timing and the details to the Lord. This is what He has instructed us to do: "Be still, and know that I am God" (Psalm 46:10). This has been and will always be the source of true peace.

All who know God has a home and an authorized prophet on earth need have no great concern about the timing and circumstances of various events. When the *if*'s are gone and we know the Savior lives and loves us and will be our final judge, we live our lives far differently from the way those (including ourselves at times when we forget) who do not know this and still harbor *if*'s in their hearts.

After seeing and feeling these things, I was almost embarrassed by my concerns over this particular, relatively small, restoration project. I continued to feel the Lord's encouragement to keep trying, however, so I did. I appreciated the help from many in the Church's Temple Department and tried to be more patient and believing, especially when things slowed way down. I still got frustrated at times and returned again and again to prayer and scriptures for solace.

At one point the issue of funding was raised as a possible holdup. I quickly assured those at Church headquarters that if asked, the local members would gladly contribute whatever was needed. We knew that President Hinckley would need to approve the restoration, as well as the funding, so we prayed for him, gave our input, and continued to wait in faith.

After what seemed a long time, President Hinckley did approve the restoration and asked us to raise all of the needed funds locally. What joy filled our hearts! We simply let the stake presidents, ordinance workers, patrons, and other interested individuals from our temple district know of this opportunity. We set no quotas. And the money began to accumulate. Some donated to honor their pioneer ancestors, others donated to express gratitude for the blessings of the temple to their families past, present, and future. Many, including older widows and widowers, wept in gratitude for the privilege of contributing their mite to help restore that which had been temporarily lost. Hundreds contributed in both large and small amounts. There was a rather short deadline, but when the time arrived, substantially more than the required amount was submitted to the Church.

The long-awaited restoration finally began. It included reopening the ceiling to nearly its original height, reopening and restoring the four original windows, which had been closed for more than sixty years, adding exquisite art glass, and extending the existing murals upward so the sky and clouds reached as it were all the way to heaven. The project also included the installation of a new chandelier especially designed for that sacred room, extensive gold leafing and accenting, new carpeting, new furnishings, and many other

*Celestial room of
the Idaho Falls temple
after the restoration of
original features.*

enhancements. Heaven's blessings were over the restoration, and when it was finished, the room was very close to its original design. God let us know that the original builders were pleased and that He himself smiled upon it.

When the temple reopened, large throngs of grateful people experienced marvelous outpourings of the Spirit. Jean and I attended a session the first day, and as we entered the celestial room our eyes and thoughts, along with those of other patrons, were drawn up, up, up—all the way, as it were, to heaven. Everyone was wrapped in quiet reverence. I saw many searching, tearful eyes gazing heavenward, and the awe I had felt as an eleven-year-old child returned with even added power. As I gazed upward, the thrill of truth coursed through my soul, and I seemed to hear the Lord speaking from the scriptures:

"[I] restore again that which was lost" (D&C 124:28).

"They shall be restored unto the knowledge of their fathers" (2 Nephi 30:5).

"I restore all things" (D&C 132:45).

I returned to my office and asked to be left alone for a while. As I gave thanks for and contemplated the beauty of that special "restored" room, I received a sure witness that its specialness came from the Spirit of the Lord. The gold leafing, the new art glass for the windows, and every other enhancement were only earthly reminders of His eternal power and beauty.

I knew the room itself was not very large and that there are thousands of rooms much larger, more opulent, and with higher ceilings. To God, physical measurements are not of great importance. The Kirtland Temple was not very large, yet the restorations that took place there are beyond compare. Our homes may not be very large or fancy, yet they are among the most important places on earth because many of the greatest events of eternal significance take place there. The stable in Bethlehem was not very large, but it was where the Savior was born and from where He went forth to accomplish that which is of the greatest possible eternal significance. Temples generally are not the largest, most lavish buildings on earth, but outside of the home, they are the most important because they are where God abides and where people are moved or restored to higher spheres of existence.

As I continued to ponder, pray, read scriptures, and give thanks for the great blessing of this restoration, I began to see that in an important sense all good things are restorations.

Having the gospel on the earth today is a restoration (see Acts 3:21). The resurrection is a restoration (see Alma 41:2). Forgiveness is a restoration (see Alma 41:13). A testimony is a restoration (see Moroni 9:36). The covenants and truths of the temple are restorations. The latter-day gathering of Israel is a restoration (see D&C 84:2). The understanding of truth is largely a restoration of that which we have known before but may have forgotten (see D&C 124:28). In fact, I came to understand that essentially everything we need for our eternal progress is in some way a restoration.

I wondered, *Can something be restored to us that we have never had?* Those who were faithful in their first estate were given a body, whereas those who were not faithful did not receive a body. Those given a body, will, after death, have it restored in the resurrection; those who were unfaithful have no body to be restored. So desperately do Satan and his hosts want bodies that they gladly go into swine, even if but for a moment! They know they can never fully have our bodies, but they continue to try to influence us to do things that harm our bodies and to do evil so they can have some control over our bodies for a while.

What a blessing to have a body and what a blessing to know that by our obedience to God, Satan can be kept away from it. Many have challenges in this life with their minds and bodies, but it is wonderful to know that in the resurrection, our minds and bodies will be restored to their perfect state—or "original design."

A good part of this life consists of having things we value and then losing them and wanting them back. All of us have lost something, physical or spiritual, that we would like

Public domain.

The Lost Coin, *by James Tissot.*

back—youth, health, memory, patience, strength, trust, love, and much more.

I believe a reason the Lord gave parables about lost coins, lost sheep, lost sons, and many more lost things (see Luke 15) is to help us understand that with His help we can find (or have restored) everything of eternal value. Of course, we must do our part by working hard, searching, repenting, praying, and being patient, loving, kind, and faithful. As we do these things and develop these qualities, everything of eternal value will be found or restored.

Alma explains, "The plan of restoration is requisite with the justice of God; for it is requisite that all things should be restored to their proper order" (Alma 41:2) and "the meaning of the word restoration is to bring back again . . . good for that which is good; righteous for that which is righteous" (Alma 41:13; see also Alma 41; 42).

How on earth (or in heaven) can we expect to have

goodness or mercy restored to us if we have not been good or merciful? How can we expect anything to be restored to us if we have never had it? What a powerful motivation this understanding of restoration is in helping us to be faithful, to have good feelings toward others, and to do good things.

As near as I can tell, all of God's commandments have the principle of restoration, or the lost being restored, embedded in them somewhere. As we continually come unto Jesus in His home, His temple, every blessing that is important in time or eternity can be found and restored to us.

The scriptures tell us that one of the reasons the gospel was restored was to save a "ruined world" (D&C 135:6). Through restorations, God saves not only ruined worlds but ruined buildings, ruined bodies, ruined lives, and ruined families. The Savior said, "And this is life eternal, that they might know thee the only true God, and Jesus Christ, whom thou hast sent" (John 17:3). To live so we can receive a restoration of this most important of all knowledge is as great a blessing as I can think of.

I continue to be overwhelmed with love and appreciation to the Lord for all of His restorations, now and in the future. I pray that we will all continue to do good things, so that through the eternal law of restoration, we can have good things restored to us. I express my endless gratitude that God has seen fit to restore to me and many others the opportunity to again feel drawn up, up, up, right into heaven. I pray that we can not only see but be transported all the way to heaven and beyond.

Chapter 19

JEWELS

Jewels are fascinating. We are drawn to them by their sparkle, color, beauty, and rarity. Though they are captivating, there is another type of jewel more valuable, more beautiful, more rare, and far more desirable, which I discovered in the temple. Here is how it happened.

With the announcement that a temple would be built in Rexburg, Idaho, there was increased excitement and activity in the Idaho Falls temple district of which Rexburg was then a part. Our temple was extremely busy, and most evenings we had difficulty accommodating all who came, but somehow we were able to do so. The First Presidency had recently approved the call of several new sealers and the releases of a few others for health reasons or to serve missions. It therefore became necessary to make significant changes in the schedules of fourteen of our sealers.

We prayerfully worked out a proposed schedule, and I was assigned to visit with those fourteen couples and see if the new times would work for them. I felt I should visit with each couple and decided to ask all of them to come at the same time to a meeting in the temple chapel. Without exception they all said they would be there.

As the day of the meeting drew near, I became increasingly concerned about the effect these changes might have on these couples. I prayed for guidance and received the following impression, which was both an assurance and a gentle rebuke: "These are my sealers. They have been tried and tested. Don't worry about them. All will be well."

When the meeting began, I found myself looking into the faces of twenty-eight smiling people all dressed in white. I felt as beautiful a spirit as I have ever felt from any group anywhere. I knew I was looking into the faces of some of God's most valiant souls. They glowed with love and devotion.

I outlined the need for the changes and asked that each couple (in alphabetical order) to come to a private place in the back of the chapel where we would discuss their proposed new schedule. I asked them to be forthright about any health or personal concerns so we could make any needed adjustments. I specifically asked that each wife give her input, as I wanted to be sure she felt good about the new schedule. When their interview was over, I asked each couple to return to the chapel and wait with the group, so we could make any additional adjustments that might be needed. I hoped I had blocked out enough time to make the necessary changes.

The first few couples accepted their assignments with no changes. When I got to the fourth couple, the wife said that she had recently been called as a ward Relief Society president and was concerned about her schedule. When I showed them their proposed schedule, she smiled and said, "That's exactly the time I was going to request. It fits my schedule perfectly."

When we got down to the last three couples and still had no changes, I began to wonder, *Is it possible that everyone is going to accept their schedule with no changes?* I hadn't believed that could happen and still wasn't sure; however, when the last couple gave the same response as all the others—"That is fine, President. That time will work well for us"—I could hardly believe it. Not a single exception. Twenty-eight busy people—all of one heart and one mind! As the reality of what had just happened sank in, a light of understanding began to shine in my mind, and I saw things I had not seen before.

I returned to the chapel, thanked the workers for their patience, and explained that since everyone had accepted their assignment exactly as proposed, there was no need for additional changes, so we would not need to stay longer. I saw twenty-eight quiet nods and smiles, which seemed to say to me, *What else did you expect?* I expressed my love for each of them and bore my testimony with a slight catch in my voice and a little fog in my eyes. I was overwhelmed with their faithfulness and knew that I was looking into the faces of some of God's most noble men and women.

When everyone had left, I saw that the time I had blocked out for the meeting, including the anticipated further changes, was not nearly used up, so I stayed in the chapel to ponder what had just happened. As I was marveling at the faithfulness of those humble, obedient people, a verse of scripture came to my mind: "Yet I will own them, and they shall be mine in that day when I shall come to make up my jewels" (D&C 101:3).

It came with great force to me that right there in that very room, in that temple, that day, I had witnessed the luster of some of God's brightest jewels! What a privilege. I bowed my head in deep gratitude for the blessing of seeing them as God sees them. A thought flashed through my mind that maybe this is one of the ways the universe is run—everyone doing what they are asked to do, when and how they are asked to do it, no exceptions.

Those feelings stayed with me, and each succeeding day in the temple I saw more and more shimmering jewels and wondered why I had not seen them before. What a humbling experience to realize that right before my eyes I was witnessing the daily celestial refining of faithful, obedient souls into brilliant jewels for God's crown!

I continued to notice additional jewels, such as a faithful man who, though suffering from shingles, was always at his post; a faithful woman who, in spite of unrelenting back pain, continued to fill her assignments; a faithful grandmother who, though suffering from a great personal loss, persisted in exuding warmth, serenity, and testimony; and many other faithful souls who continued to reflect the luster imparted by the polishing hand of God. I could see that in submitting their wills to His, they were being buffed, polished, and refined into luminous celestial jewels. As my eyes opened wider I saw not just a few but hundreds, thousands, even an innumerable number of God's jewels reflecting celestial light from homes and temples and other sacred places throughout the world and the universe.

With this new vision, I recalled many past events in a different light. I remembered being with Jean on a busy street in front of the Manhattan New York Temple, waiting for a friend. As the throngs of humanity rushed by, I noticed that most of the people seemed solemn, burdened, and anxious to get somewhere else. I was fascinated and wondered if any of them were happy. Just then I noticed a young African American man who began to separate from the crowds. There was something different about his appearance and demeanor—he walked more purposefully and had a certain enthusiastic yet serene aura about him. As he neared the entrance of the building, he completely departed from the crowd and with a giant, unforgettable smile entered the temple. Soon our friend arrived, and we also entered the temple. Before long I saw that same giant smile glowing from the face of that man, who now stood before us as an ordinance worker.

I remembered individuals and experiences in temples, in homes, and in missionary and other meetings in such diverse places as Hawaii, Argentina, Tonga, Hong Kong, Europe, Utah, Idaho, California, and many other locations. As I remembered those people, the luster of unnumbered jewels flashed through my mind. I saw parents tenderly caring for handicapped children, husbands or wives lovingly nursing spouses who are sick or otherwise incapacitated, individuals patiently helping aged parents or grandparents, missionaries faithfully preaching the gospel, others valiantly defending freedom, and on and on. What a blessing to know that God's jewels are being polished wherever righteous men and women, who know and love the Lord, are anxiously engaged in His work of blessing the lives of His children.

A few days later a good brother knocked on my door, introduced himself as the bishop of a ward in an older part of town, and asked if we could visit for a moment. He was very discouraged and said that their ward had planned for weeks to come to the temple this evening, but only he and two others had shown up. He asked, "Where are all the solid, faithful, 'Martin's Cove' type Saints today? I sure need some in my ward."

I assured him that there are faithful people all around us who come to the temple regularly and help in any way they can. Some come long distances, over challenging roads, and through difficult weather conditions. Some come from close by. Some are older, some are younger, some are healthy, some are not, yet they come, grateful for the privilege of serving in the Lord's house. I reminded him that there are faithful people in every ward and stake, including his.

"I guess so," he said, "but I wonder who they are. I wish they would identify themselves."

I reminded him that God's jewels never call attention to themselves because that would be contrary to the very nature of heaven—but that the Savior had said, "By their fruits ye shall know them" (Matthew 7:20). I explained further that it is our responsibility to open our spiritual eyes and see them; it is not their responsibility to tell us who they are. As humble individuals draw closer to the Savior, the more quietly they go about helping others, never seeking the limelight or expecting honors.

I explained a little about what I had been experiencing in noticing jewels everywhere. I told him of my belief that each person is a latent jewel, needing only to be smoothed, refined, and polished so he or she can radiate his or her unique color and reflect the light of the gospel. I testified that there were humble people in his ward, as in all wards and all nations and among all peoples, who had some degree of luster, and that it is our duty as leaders and under-shepherds to identify that glow and find ways to help them maximize it. He

聖徒教育

"AND THEY SHALL BE MINE, SAID THE LORD OF HOSTS, IN THAT DAY WHEN I MAKE UP MY JEWELS; AND I WILL SPARE THEM, AS A MAN SPARETH HIS OWN SON THAT SERVETH HIM.

...IN THAT DAY WHEN I SHALL COME TO MAKE UP MY JEWELS."

nodded in agreement and left. I noticed a slight smile on his face, even though I wasn't certain I had fully succeeded in helping him deal with his disappointment.

Afterward, I gave some additional thought to this topic. I reflected on the many faithful couples and single individuals whom I observed regularly coming to serve in the temple. Many came in spite of trying circumstances or failing health, some carrying heavy emotional burdens or filled with sorrow and disappointment. And yet they came—trusting in the Lord, eager to show their love for Him by fulfilling what they felt to be their duty, seeking to receive strength from Him, and yes, even though unconsciously, coming to be honed and tempered and polished as jewels fitted for God's crown and kingdom.

I remembered Mormon, who in a time of terrible wars, suffering, and wickedness, was still able to say:

"Wherefore, I would speak unto you that are of the church, that are the peaceable followers of Christ, and that have obtained a sufficient hope by which ye can enter into the rest of the Lord, from this time henceforth until ye shall rest with him in heaven. And now my brethren, I judge these things of you because of your peaceable walk with the children of men. For I remember the word of God which saith by their works ye shall know them; for if their works be good, then they are good also" (Moroni 7:3–5).

I could better relate to the words of John the Revelator when he said: "What are these which are arrayed in white robes? And whence came they? . . . These are they which came out of great tribulation, and have washed their robes, and made them white in the blood of the Lamb. Therefore are they before the throne of God, and serve him day and night in his temple: and he that sitteth on the throne shall dwell among them" (Revelation 7:13–15).

I also felt increased love for the words given to Malachi: "And they shall be mine, saith the Lord of hosts, in that day when I make up my jewels" (Malachi 3:17).

And for the words given to the Prophet Joseph Smith: "For I, the Lord, rule in the heavens above, and among the armies of the earth; and in the day when I shall make up my jewels, all men shall know what it is that bespeaketh the power of God" (D&C 60:4).

Yes, jewels are forged in the furnaces of affliction, with much patience, over long periods of time, yet jewels are what God wants us to become. Only as polished jewels can we experience the joy that comes from being an integral part of His crown and His kingdom.

I know that jewels are forged in places other than temples, but it was in the temple I first began to see them sparkle as they were being refined, purged, and purified. I thrill to know that there are many walking the earth today who could comfortably walk the streets of Enoch's city and feel right at home in that Zion! I hope we may be among them.

Chapter 20

THE GREAT LEVELER

One evening a man asked if he could visit with me. He said he had been a schoolteacher and administrator all of his life and considered himself to be active in the Church. For years he had held a secret grudge toward some business and professional people who, he felt, didn't work as hard nor contribute as much to society as he did, yet they made more money. He quietly resented that he struggled financially while they had larger homes, better cars, and more comfortable lives.

He continued, "Recently I began attending the temple more regularly. Not long ago I was in a certain place with a particular person when I realized that against my better desires, I was actually harboring some unkind feelings towards that person. I immediately began to repent and seek forgiveness. I hadn't realized what a withering effect this subtle animosity had been having on my spirit. I do not want to have these or any other unkind or unholy feelings towards others. What can I do? Do you think it is too late?"

I was impressed with his humility and sincerity and told him that it is never too late, that God loves him and would help him, and that through the Savior and His temple, he could eventually become fully clean and pure and rid himself of unkind thoughts. I explained that eternity is a long time, and because he was on the right path, if he continued to keep his covenants, all would be well.

He listened without speaking as he contemplated these truths. He finally looked up and trembling slightly, whispered, "Then it isn't too late? You think I really can be rid of these bad feelings?"

"That's right," I said. "Let me share some scriptures with you."

We then read the following together:

"Verily, verily, I say unto you, my servants, that insomuch as you have forgiven one another your trespasses, even so I, the Lord, forgive you" (D&C 82:1). I told him that I felt part of forgiving one another was for him to forgive himself when he truly repented. He nodded in agreement.

We then read: "Behold and lo, mine eyes are upon you, and the heavens and the earth are in mine hands, and the riches of eternity are mine to give" (D&C 67:2). I told him that the keys to these riches are found in the temple, so if he continued to attend and serve and learn and live the truths taught there, he would eventually have all he could hope for and more. He assured me that he would keep coming and remain faithful.

Then he said: "For all these years I've had it wrong on wealth and riches. I thought there was an unfair gap and resented it. Now I see that where it counts there is no disparity. In the Lord's temple, everyone has the same opportunity regardless of their financial or social standing. Here it is clear that in the Lord's sight, everyone is equal and the riches of eternity are available to all. Why didn't I see that before?"

We visited a little more, and he left feeling greatly encouraged. I marveled at what a blessing the temple had been in opening his eyes and helping him change his heart. What a great leveler and revealer and helper the temple is to those who listen. In His love and fairness, God gives everyone the same opportunity to seek the riches of eternity, which is really all that counts. All of us can have these riches as soon as we achieve the spiritual attributes and maturity needed to use them properly. We learn how to gain those attributes and develop that maturity in the temple, where the process is clearly outlined. As I thought about this opportunity being open to all, I felt a desire to attend an endowment session.

As I waited for the session to begin and watched the patrons gathering, I saw many people with whom I was acquainted. I noticed a mayor, a wealthy businessman, and several teachers—some from humble circumstances and others from more prosperous conditions. Some had light skin, some dark, some were men, some were women, some were younger, some older, two were in wheelchairs, and one was blind. Despite these differences, each had qualified in the same way and had come to serve, to learn, and to grow.

Everyone was quiet, reverent, helpful, and respectful. All were dressed the same, followed the same procedures, received the same promises, and were treated in the same way. Wealth or lack thereof, position in society, race, age, or health were of no consequence. The officiator was a rather small man from humble circumstances, but everyone paid close attention to him and followed his direction, demonstrating their understanding that he was serving as an

Detail from *The Eternal Family through Christ*, by Judith Mehr. Courtesy Intellectual Reserve, Inc.

Equal before God.

authorized servant of the Lord. Each person in that session (and hopefully all sessions) loved God, was striving to keep his or her covenants, and was working to live righteously. Each was a welcome guest in the Lord's house. Observing the people in that company, it struck me that Peter had spoken well when he said, "Of a truth I perceive that God is no respecter of persons: But in every nation he that feareth him, and worketh righteousness, is accepted with him" (Acts 10:34–35). It was clear to me that in the temple all are equal in the sight of God.

When the session ended, I went to my office and marveled at what I had just experienced. I could see how the temple was not only a great leveler but a great unifier, revealer, healer, and exalter. Through temple service, we become more humble, more obedient, more helpful, more charitable, more faithful—in short, we become more Christlike, more able to properly handle the riches of eternity.

What a remarkable thing it is that at birth we come from the presence of God, after death we can return to His presence, and while here in mortality we can be in His presence in His temple. It is obvious God loves us and wants to be around us and have us around Him! Just think: In every realm of existence we are taught the same eternal principles that will allow us to be with Him eternally and enjoy it! How wonderful to know that in His presence, including in the temple, we are seen not for our wealth or power or position but for our humility, our love, our obedience, our faithfulness, and our desire to help others—all qualities needed to properly use the riches of eternity.

I thought of my earlier conversation with the school teacher and how the things of this world often do seem important to us. Think of movies and books filled with stories of pirates, detectives, intrigue, and people paying terrible prices to get clues and signs and keys to unlock worldly treasures of gold and silver, which if obtained last but a moment. God has infinitely more wealth and power than there is in this entire world. He wants to share all of it with us. In His temple He freely gives us all the clues, signs, and directions needed to find and receive that greatest treasure of all—the riches of eternity. What an unselfish plan! Just learn and follow the teachings of the temple, and when we become sufficiently humble, kind, obedient, and faithful so we can properly handle them, they are given to us! And they last forever!

I was still contemplating these truths when I heard a soft knock and looked up to see an ordinance worker with a faraway look in his eyes. I motioned him to come in.

He whispered, "President, can I tell you of an experience I just had while serving at the recommend desk this evening? At the end of a short line of people waiting to enter the temple, I saw a man I had been friends with in my youth and thought to myself, *That looks like George, but it couldn't be. There is no way he could be in the temple.* Even though both George and I were a little rebellious in high school, George really went off the deep end.

"When he got closer, there was no question—it *was* George! Oh, how I prayed for help! When he got to the desk, he smiled and handed me his recommend. I looked at it, saw that it was in order, and began to tremble. What should I do? Then I remembered the instruction we had received to accept all valid recommends because it is the bishops and stake presidents who determine worthiness to enter the temple, not us. A feeling of relief came over me and I said, 'Welcome to the temple, George. I never thought I would see *you* here.' He looked at me and replied, 'And Bill, I never thought I would see *you* here.'

"Even though I knew I was not supposed to leave my station, I stepped around the desk, embraced George, and whispered, 'Isn't it marvelous that because of the Savior and repentance it is possible for both of us to be in the temple?'

"Tears flowed freely as we held each other for a moment. Those in line didn't seem to mind; in fact, I saw many smiles and a few with tears as George entered the temple. My original judgmental feelings toward George (and hopefully, his toward me) were completely gone. Amazing! George and I both in God's temple!"

Filled with a wonderful spirit of gratitude, the worker testified, "How gracious of the Lord to promise that He will be the final judge, and we don't need to worry about those decisions. What a blessing! He gives us the easy part and keeps the hard part. We just check the recommend, and God does the rest. I can't get over it—George in the temple, clean and worthy. Who would have thought? And me not only here but serving as a worker. Amazing! I hope I did right. I feel I did."

I assured him he had.

As the day ended, I contemplated the events that had taken place. I thought of Bill's and George's reunion. It was as though I could see their embrace and feel their joy. Then that embrace seemed to stretch into eternity and be repeated endless times as I remembered the Lord's promise to Enoch and his people: "We will receive them into our bosom, and they shall see us; and we will fall upon their necks, and they shall fall upon our necks, and we will kiss each other" (Moses 7:63).

I felt such a deep love for our Savior and His atoning sacrifice and resurrection, with their promises of forgiveness and immortality, that for a period of time, I could hardly move. I remembered Bill's words about the Judgment, where God gives us the easy part and keeps the hard part. I realized that the same is true of the Savior's atonement and the resurrection.

Just as Jesus was comforted and strengthened in His hour of greatest need, so will He comfort and strengthen us (see Luke 22:43). He gives us the easy part and keeps the hard part. All we have to do to receive the blessings of the Atonement is have faith and repent. He did the hard part and

Courtesy Visual Resources Library, The Church of Jesus Christ of Latter-day Saints.

Gethsemane, *by Carl Bloch.*

paid the ultimate price. If we ever think repentance is hard, or we feel we have been treated badly by others, just think how that is absolutely nothing compared to what the Savior went through. Think of what He did, and continues to do, for each of us. No matter how hard death may seem, it is nothing compared to what He went through in His life and on the cross to bring about the resurrection. And still, He is always willing and eager to help us in every needful way!

I thought of the schoolteacher who was learning great lessons and making important changes and of the session I had attended with its marvelous "leveling" effect. I remembered when Jean and I went to a temple session with all the General Authorities and their wives shortly after being called to that body. I was humbled and excited to see

President Spencer W. Kimball and the other leaders, all of whom I greatly loved and respected. But when I entered the waiting room, suddenly my only concern was to find Jean. I still loved and respected everyone in the room, but to me Jean was the most important person there. Being awestruck in the presence of famous people may be part of this life, but in the temple we understand who and what is most important. In the temple we stand individually, not only before the Lord but before our loved ones and families from both sides of the veil. Jean has never been more important to me or loved more by me than in the temple!

In my mind I saw many people in many places, speaking many languages, over many eras of time, all coming to the temple, all learning eternal truths, all dedicating their lives to building the kingdom of God and all sharing equally in the riches of eternity. Because the teachings, authority, covenants, and ordinances of the temple are from God, they are eternal and unchanging throughout the universe, regardless of language, race, culture, or time.

It doesn't matter, then, what particular circumstance or role we are given in life, or what our credentials might be outside of the temple, or even what our past behavior might have been. It only matters that we are worthily in the temple, making sacred promises, and striving with all of our hearts to keep those promises.

Yes, the temple is a great leveler, the ultimate unifier, the great revealer, the great healer, the great restorer, the great exalter, and the key to obtaining the riches of eternity. The comfort and peace these eternal truths brought me were the perfect ending to that beautiful day in the house of the Lord.

Chapter 21

MOM? DAD?

A stake president called and asked about bringing an older gentleman and his wife to the temple to receive their endowments, to be sealed to each other, and for the man to be sealed to his deceased parents. He noted that the man had terminal cancer and would be in a wheelchair. I replied that if the man and his family members had valid recommends, they were welcome to come anytime and that our ordinance workers and sealers would handle the physical logistics. He assured me that they both had current recommends and were ready and anxious to come. The president also mentioned that this couple had been members of the Church for many years but had only recently become active with the help of home teachers who had taken a genuine interest in them. We made an appointment.

We had to postpone that initial appointment because the brother was hospitalized. After a week, the doctors released him from the hospital to go home and be with his wife and family, informing them that further treatment would do him no good. The stake president called and said that the man was still anxious to come to the temple but he could no longer use a wheelchair—he would have to come on a hospital gurney. I reiterated that as long as he and his wife came with valid recommends, we would handle the rest.

When I told the shift coordinator what to expect, he smiled and said that since this was the Lord's work, all would be well. I knew my confidence in the workers and their confidence in the Lord would be fully justified.

In a few hours the party arrived: the man on a gurney, his wife in a wheelchair, along with a few family members, the stake president, the bishop, the faithful home teachers, and some other friends from the ward.

A few hours later I met this group of radiant patrons in one of the sealing rooms. The brother was still strapped to his hospital gurney but fully awake and smiling. He expressed his love and appreciation to the Lord and to the workers for all they had done to accommodate him. There was a heavenly spirit of peace and love as he and his wife were sealed to each other and when the man's parents were sealed by proxy to each other.

It was now time to seal him to his parents. It was obvious that his faith, love, and desire were as strong as ever but that his body was getting weaker. I asked if he felt he could proceed. The light in his eyes shone even more brightly as he whispered, "Yes—oh, yes."

Someone helped him place his hand on the hands of the proxies for his parents and as the simple but powerful words were pronounced, I noticed tears flowing from his closed eyes. As the last amen was said, he opened his eyes as though gazing directly into heaven. I saw his lips move slightly and distinctly heard him whisper, "Mom? Dad?"

I was close enough to tell that this was not just a question but a statement of fact. The words were uttered so softly that most in the room could not hear them. However, everyone who needed to hear, including many from the other side, heard and understood perfectly. The look of love and joy and serenity that enveloped him was so powerful that everyone in the room was moved to tears. It would be hard to imagine a more spiritual and reverent moment.

With the eternally essential work now complete, family members, friends, and temple workers helped the couple prepare for their trip home. As they departed, the couple told me they had been given such loving care, they felt as though they were in heaven with angels attending them. I told them that this was in fact the case.

A few days later the man's stake president called and informed me that this brother had quietly passed away in his sleep. His wife, some family members, and a few others had been at his side as he made the peaceful transition from this mortal life to the next. The stake president expressed gratitude for all who had helped them in the temple and said the couple had left the temple feeling so fulfilled, so happy, and so at peace that they had no fear of death. When the brother passed on, they knew that in addition to family and friends at his bedside were family and friends waiting to welcome him on the other side as he passed through the veil.

When I hung up the phone, an overpowering feeling of assurance enveloped me, and for a moment I was back in the sealing room, seeing and hearing that soft whisper: "Mom? Dad?" It was given me to understand that his now being with his mom and dad on the other side was no less real than his being with them in that sealing room a few days earlier.

Accounts in the Old Testament often indicate that when

Detail from The Purpose of Life, *by Robert Oliver Skemp.*

a person died, he was gathered to his people or to his fathers (Genesis 25:8; 35:29, etc.). In the New Testament parable, after dying, the poor man Lazarus was described as being carried "into Abraham's bosom" (Luke 16:22). On the cross, as Jesus finished His mortal life, He cried, "Father, into thy hands I commend my spirit" (Luke 23:46).

We may not have the same experience in the temple as this brother had, but I have learned that in the temple we can feel a closeness to righteous ancestors or other family members who can give us a sense of connection and an assurance of help that transcends time and space. With this assurance we can receive the confidence and strength needed to continue our journey toward them and the celestial glory of God.

Since the temple is a bit of heaven on earth, we don't need to wait until we die to go to heaven; we just need to go to the temple with the proper spirit. When we are in the temple with the spirit of love, gratitude, and a determination to obey God, there is little difference between here and there. Jesus came to earth with a spirit of love, gratitude, and a determination to obey His Father and thus was both on earth and in heaven. When we go to His house with that same spirit, we begin to comprehend what heaven is.

Though the temple is one of the best places to feel a closeness to our departed, faithful family members, those connections can be felt with them at other times and places. While serving as a young missionary on a small island at a particularly lonely and discouraging time, I felt the presence of one of my grandfathers. Even though he had died before I was born, I instinctively knew who he was and received great comfort and encouragement from the depth of his smile and the warmth of his love. Church President George Albert Smith told of having a similar experience with his grandfather George A. Smith, who came to him in a dream and said, "I would like to know what you have done with my name."[1]

No matter who we are or what we might know of our parents or other ancestors, we all have a wonderful heritage to draw upon, which includes Abraham, Isaac, and Jacob— all fathers of the faithful. If we have faith even as small as a mustard seed—which we have if we are able to qualify for a temple recommend—then we can know that these great forefathers and many others want us to feel our connection to them and know that they are eager to help us. More than one person has been able to cry out "Mom? Dad?" and receive the help and peace they needed to continue to move forward in this life or to move on to the next one.

Understanding the connection between heaven and earth gives meaning to life and death. The veil is thin, and those on the other side are as real as those here.

Chapter 22

REFUGE

It was cold and dark, and a chill wind was blowing as Sister Groberg and I made our way to the temple through driving snow at 4:15 one morning. We wondered how many people would brave the raging elements to be in the temple that early hour. But when we entered, we were greeted by dozens of faithful workers ready to serve. I marveled at their courage and faith in coming long distances through difficult conditions to be at their assigned stations. The glow of faith coming from them, along with the warmth and light in the temple, were a stark contrast to the cold and darkness of the world outside.

As I looked at those faithful workers, I received an impression that beyond the physical storms blowing outside, there were other storms blowing in some of their hearts—storms of disappointment, storms of health concerns, storms of financial need, or other stormy challenges. Despite these storms, they had come in faith and were at peace, for the Lord had made His temple "a refuge from the storm" (D&C 115:6).

As I visited with several individuals who, I knew, were

in the midst of personal trials or storms, I felt a celestial radiance from them that is difficult to describe but easy to feel. I talked with a sister who just days earlier had lost her husband. I expressed surprise at seeing her back so soon and asked how she was doing. She replied that she was at peace and was exactly where she wanted to be—at her station. She was sure her husband would be at his station on the other side and assured me they would be closer to each other at their stations than anywhere else. What vision! What faith!

I visited with several others who were dealing with various other problems. Each expressed unwavering faith and gratitude for being in the temple. I knew that this bit of heaven on earth had become a "strength to the needy in his distress, a refuge from the storm" (Isaiah 25:4).

Throughout the day I pondered on how the temple was truly a refuge from storms for those on both sides of the veil. Many on this side were finding peace by helping those on the other side find peace as they were released from whatever storms of bondage they were in. I remembered the Savior's promise that we are forgiven even as we forgive (see Matthew 6:12) and wondered if similarly we may be released from our own storms as we help release others from theirs.

It became clear that since Jesus has overcome all things, He is the refuge from every storm for everyone everywhere in every situation. Since He is always in His temple, it is easy to see why it is the ultimate refuge from every storm. The psalmist expressed it well when he said, "God is our refuge and strength, a very present help in trouble" (Psalm 46:1).

Think of the strength and blessings gained by overcoming storms. There are places in Idaho that have a reputation for being very cold in the winter, with lots of snow and

Image by Valerie Ann Anderson. Courtesy of The Church of Jesus Christ of Latter-day Saints. Used by permission.

Storm clouds over the Kansas City Missouri temple.

ice and wind. Some people complain about the snow and cold and wind but never about the resulting clean air and the clean water from the life-giving rivers—or even the great missionaries developed under those harsh conditions. Just as the earth is cleansed and refreshed through storms, so can we be cleansed and refreshed in our own lives if we seek out the Lord's refuge while facing our personal storms.

Sometimes we shy away from callings or responsibilities because we think they may be too hard, forgetting that the very inconvenience or difficulty of those callings may be the exact spiritual wind or snow or cold we need to clear our vision, prove our mettle, strengthen our resolve, and increase our faith. Earthly storms help to clean the air we breathe and the water we drink. The same principles apply spiritually. Taking on difficult tasks and receiving the Lord's help not only opens our eyes but also nourishes our souls and gives us courage to face other storms that may come our way. If we shrink from tough situations, we also pull away from the growth, strength, and understanding those situations provide.

Because of God's love for us and His understanding that growth comes from overcoming storms, He allows and probably even orchestrates parts of our lives to be tough, so we can develop the qualities we need to become more like Him. President David O. McKay said, "There is no development of character without resistance; there is no growth of spirituality without overcoming."[1]

Thus, there will always be storms to pass through in this life. Getting through these storms with God's help develops patience, testimony, strength, compassion, and understanding, which we could achieve in no other way. God always has and always will provide a sure refuge from these storms for those who seek it.

I remember as a young missionary learning great lessons by going through rough waters, lessons I could not have learned by going through smooth waters. Once, we were caught in the middle of a big storm, and our boat was capsized. I was thrown into the churning ocean and had difficulty keeping my head above water. When the worst of the storm had passed, I saw that the shore was still a long way off. I was getting quite discouraged when suddenly I heard a happy cry from one of my shipmates who was between me and the shore. He had found a submerged rock and was standing on it with his head above water!

Excitedly, I made my way to him. Soon my feet touched that solid rock, and I too stood with my head slightly above water. You can perhaps imagine the thrill that passed through me as I stood there. That brief moment of standing on solid rock brought me both physical and emotional relief and gave me the needed determination and strength to continue swimming to shore. Even though the swells were still heavy and the shore a long way off, I was now filled with hope. Before the sun went down, I had made it to shore.

Remembering that storm, my discouragement and exhaustion before the rock, and my hope and energy after the rock brought a flood of testimony to me. Jesus is the Rock of our Salvation, and all who build or stand on Him will not drown but will make it to shore (see Psalm 62:7; see also 1 Nephi 13:36; 3 Nephi 11:39; Matthew 7:24; 1 Peter 2:4–8).

Places of refuge are important because some storms can be devastating, even deadly, without them. When the Israelites reached the promised land, God told Moses to provide cities of refuge where people in trouble could flee and find protection (see Numbers 35:11–12). I used to move rapidly through those parts of the Old Testament, but now they have become very meaningful to me.

All of us are guilty of some sin and need somewhere to flee for protection. The Savior is the great protector. Flee to Him! In our day, His home, the temple, is to me our "city of refuge." It is the place to which we can flee and find safety and protection in understanding and forgiveness and where the avenger is kept away, as long as we are trying to do better.

In our temple refuge, we can regroup, recommit, and find and receive the needed strength to move forward in the Lord. Isaiah said: "And there shall be a tabernacle [a temple] for a shadow in the daytime from the heat, and for a place of refuge, and for a covert from storm and from rain" (Isaiah 4:6).

As I thought of this, I thought of the many people who find refuge in the temple each day, not only from stormy weather but also from personal and family storms—storms of doubt and fear and uncertainty. I know there are other places of refuge, such as prayer, scripture study, sacrament meetings, family, friends, and listening to and obeying God's servants, but if we are sincere, all of these lead us to the Lord's house—His city of refuge—His holy temple.

As we overcome challenges with the Lord's help, we grow, gain a good work ethic, and are better equipped to handle the next challenge. Too often lives of ease produce under-achieving people, whereas lives filled with challenges produce high achievers with a can-do attitude. There is a reason the scriptures describe those who are ready to enter the celestial city: "What are these which are arrayed in white robes? And whence came they? . . . These are they which *came out of great tribulation*" (Revelation 7:13, 14; emphasis added).

Coming to the temple, even through trying circum-stances, brings great blessings. When we enter the temple and focus on the Savior by paying close attention to His words, seeking His help, and sincerely trying to help others, the storms of life cease to exist for that time. When we leave the temple, the force of those storms is abated, if not elimi-nated, largely because of the expanded eternal perspective we have gained. Seeing things through the eyes of eternity, or having an eternal perspective, cuts through most storms and is a powerful healing balm from most worldly ills.

When Jean and I left the temple that day, the wind was still blowing, the snow was still falling, the temperature was still freezing, but none of that mattered to us as we seemed to float rather than trudge home. We knew the Lord was in His temple, and it would always be a sure refuge from every storm of every kind, not only for us but for all who enter therein.

Chapter 23

ALL IS WELL

A bishop called and said his ward was coming that evening for a chapel meeting and an endowment session. He wondered if after the session, he, his wife, and a sister from his ward who was having a very hard time could meet with me.

He explained that this sister had two sons and a daughter, who were all married. A few months before, her husband had unexpectedly passed away, and then just a few weeks later, her only daughter lost her only son. In each case a very brief illness had been followed by death. The woman who had experienced these two losses had prayed that the lives of both her husband and her grandson would be spared, but in spite of her prayers, both had died. The bishop said his ward member was now questioning her own faith and wondering if the Lord had abandoned her.

The bishop had assured her that the Lord loved her and her family and explained these deaths were simply a part of life, not a judgment on her. He had asked her to come with the ward to the temple, but she said she didn't feel she could go right then. He felt strongly that she should come and promised her that she would receive comfort and understanding from being in the temple. He also promised that they could meet with the temple president after the session. She hesitated and then replied, "Bishop, I trust you. I will come."

After making these Spirit-prompted promises, he felt an extra weight of responsibility and was grateful when I said I would be happy to meet with them.

That evening the bishop and many ward members came to the chapel meeting, where I was on duty. It was easy to tell who the distraught grandmother was. I was impressed that despite her obvious emotional struggles, she remained reverent and thoughtful. I could feel the Lord's love and compassion for her.

After the opening hymn and prayer, the bishop bore a beautiful testimony of the Savior and of His temple. He then turned the time to me. I had been praying about what I should say to these wonderful members and especially to this grieving sister. I felt impressed to bear my testimony of the Savior and of His ability to heal broken health, broken hearts, broken lives, and broken souls. I assured all present that the Lord loved them, wanted to help them, and was appreciative of their faithfulness for being in the temple—supporting one another and selflessly serving others. I testified that despite the challenges they might have, He always fulfills His promises to the faithful in His own time and way. I then read this comforting scripture, describing how things will be at some point in the future:

"And God shall wipe away all tears from their eyes; and there shall be no more death, neither sorrow, nor crying, neither shall there be any more pain: for the former things are passed away" (Revelation 20:4).

After reading that verse I felt impressed to ask that we sing a closing hymn, even though one was not normally scheduled in such meetings. The chorister and organist quickly conferred and chose the hymn "Come, Come, Ye Saints," presumably because it was July and the words were familiar to all there. After the singing, the ward members went on to the endowment session, and I returned to my office.

During the chapel meeting, I had sensed the nervousness of the bishop and the tender emotions of the grandmother and wondered what the Lord would have me say when they came to my office. I began to think about the blessings of being in the temple where the Lord literally has a place to "lay his head" (Matthew 8:20) and where He has promised to "manifest [himself] to [his] people in mercy" (D&C 110:7). I thought of how anxious He is to share knowledge and truth with us as soon as we are able to receive it and how our ability to receive truth increases each time we attend the temple. I realized that as we keep our temple covenants, we become stronger spiritually and can give others the assurance that they can receive the strength they need in the same way. I prayed for the bishop and this bereaved grandmother and hoped they were receiving the strength they desired.

Just then I heard a light rap on my partly open door. I invited the bishop, his wife, and this sister to come in and be seated. When I saw them, I wondered if this was the same nervous bishop and distraught grandmother I had seen just a couple of hours earlier. There was a beautiful calmness about them that was amazing. The bishop introduced everyone and asked the grandmother if she had anything she would like to ask or say.

She looked at the bishop, at his wife, and then at me. Her calm demeanor completely washed away any concerns I might have had.

"I'm fine now," she assured us. "The Lord has let me know that 'all is well.' I came tonight reluctantly, but I came because my bishop asked me to and I have always tried to obey my bishop. Before entering the temple I was not happy to be here; I was cold and shivering and filled with despair. But when I felt the warmth of the temple and the love from my ward members, I immediately felt better. The testimonies and the scriptures in our chapel meeting were wonderful; however, I didn't feel much different until we began singing the closing hymn, 'Come, Come, Ye Saints.'

"I know the words, so I started singing somewhat mechanically. But with each phrase I began to feel more peace and comfort. By the time we got to the last verse, I was feeling much more calm and warm. As we sang 'and should we die . . . ' I trembled, but in a good way, and my eyes filled with tears. And when we sang the last phrase 'all is well, all is well,' I experienced a flood of peace, warmth, and assurance. I heard, as it were, an audible voice in my heart and mind say, 'Because of the Savior, all is well. Not all *will be* well, but all *is* well.'"

She turned to her bishop and with a smile on her face said, "You don't need to worry about me anymore. I know all *is* well. Every word in the session this evening echoed in my heart: 'All *is* well—All *is* well.' I felt someone saying, 'Live faithfully—be believing—be patient—help others—keep your covenants—the Lord loves you—He knows your husband—He knows your children—He knows your grand-son—He knows you—He knows your situation—He has been there. He is both here and there. All is well here. All is well there.'"

A soft glow of peace and assurance radiated from this faithful sister, and the light of her spirit warmed us all. She concluded by saying she was grateful to be in the temple and would appreciate anything I had to say. I expressed my love for them all and bore my testimony that we were in the Lord's house and He was here helping and teaching all of us. I told the bishop that because he had obeyed the promptings of the Spirit, and the grandmother had obeyed her bishop, God had caused them both to know that all is well. I assured them that whenever we obey the promptings of the Spirit, we receive the assurance that *all is well.*

There were tears of gratitude and hugs of love as we felt an increased determination to make the temple a bigger part of our lives. We knew that in so doing we would always have the assurance that all is well and will continue to be well.

After the group left I closed the door, fell to my knees, and thanked the Lord for good bishops, for faithful members, including one special, obedient grandmother, and for the Savior—for His mission, for His house, for the understanding and testimony of eternal truths that He freely gives, and especially for the blessed assurance that because of Him, all is well.

Chapter 24

CAST YOUR BURDENS

I met the Brown family early one morning in the temple. They had just suffered a great loss but were nonetheless filled with love, testimony and gratitude.

Sometime before, their eighteen-year-old daughter, Chelsie, had been diagnosed with a rare form of cancer. She had been given priesthood blessings, and family and friends united in fasting and prayer for her. Medical procedures were begun, but despite lengthy and difficult treatments, the illness continued.

Chelsie's family and the gospel became the most important things in her life. Her family drew closer together than ever before. On one occasion she wrote in her journal:

"Sometimes, once in a while, . . . I can see a glimpse of what God sees in me, and it is so weird, but I feel grateful for the opportunity to have a trial as difficult as this. I wish I could feel like that often. I used to always kind of be bugged by the Alma the Younger story. Like when I am acting bad, God doesn't send down an angel to tell me to be good, but now it's like He is doing that for me. There I was at college being selfish and ungrateful when my life was basically easy, but now I am being shown a new perspective. God saved Alma's spiritual life, and he also saved mine, too. I used to really like my appearance and my long pretty hair, but I didn't like myself. Now, I am not too crazy about my looks, but I really like who I am on the inside. It's funny how life is like that sometimes. While all the boys my age are on missions, I'm on a mission, too. But instead, the person I am converting is myself."[1]

Chelsie's treatments were continued, but during one of them something went terribly wrong. Maybe it was miscommunication or miscalculation or lack of proper attention; probably it was a combination of them all. In any event, rather than the regular dose of medication being given, a deadly dose was administered. By the time the mistake was discovered, the death-dealing fluid had already begun to shut down parts of her body.

When Chelsie became aware of this mistake, she whispered to her father, "Dad, I want you to cuss them out good—help shake them up to make sure they are more responsible. And then let's be like the Amish and forgive them." She was referring to President James E. Faust's talk on the forgiveness that a community of Amish people had extended to a demented man who had murdered five of their children.[2]

Neither Chelsie nor her family gave up hope. She believed in the promises given her in her patriarchal blessing, which promised a great future. Members of her family stayed by her side constantly. She continued to tell them how important their family was and assured them she would be all right no matter what happened. She did all she could to encourage them to remain faithful. She slowly declined, went into a coma, and passed away not long afterward.

The Brown family with Chelsie (far right) shortly before she passed away.

What a blow to the Brown family. How should they react? What should they do? Of course there was deep mourning. Many questions were asked, sometimes with tinges of anger—as is typical of the human state. Before long, however, the unbreakable fabric of faith in the Lord, combined with the equally strong bonds of a family sealed in the temple, took control of this otherwise devastating situation, and calmness and peace prevailed.

At the family's request and with the help of many people, permission was received for Chelsie's temple work to be performed right away. Early in the morning of the day of her funeral, the Brown family went to the Idaho Falls temple, where they performed sacred ordinances for their beautiful Chelsie. My wife, Jean, was able to be with the family at the beginning of their work, and I met with them when they were ready to leave the temple. I told them I thought it was remarkable for them to be in the temple for these sacred ordinances on the very day of Chelsie's funeral.

They responded with a simple "This is where we ought to be, especially at a time like this." An aura of love and goodness and faith radiated from their countenances that I will never forget.

With those sacred ordinances completed, the family went to the funeral home, where the mother and sisters reverently dressed their beloved Chelsie in the most beautiful and meaningful manner possible in mortality. They felt whole as a family and quietly proceeded to the emotionally wrenching but faith-filled funeral service.

After Chelsie's passing, the inevitable legal issues needed to be addressed. The proceedings were complicated and frustrating, but largely because the family had decided to follow Chelsie's wish—to "cuss them out" and then "forgive them"—they eventually got through them. Each time I think of how the Brown family responded to that very difficult situation I am strengthened. What a great blessing it is to have faith and trust in the Lord and in the ordinances of His temple!

About this same time, another family with whom I was acquainted faced a similar situation. Unfortunately, their faith was not as strong, and they let anger and resentment cause them to lose their eternal perspective. Their negative attitude and resentment led to feelings of entitlement, and in their loss they continued to blame others. After spending months in court, they eventually received a large financial settlement. Over time, their physical lives returned to a semblance of normalcy, but their spiritual lives, as far as I can tell, have still not recovered.

I often think of how differently these two families responded to a similar situation. I see the Brown family with glowing countenances at peace in the temple, at the funeral home, in the chapel, at the graveside, and at their farm home. After taking time to grieve, they moved on and continue to find joy in life. They understand that their family is forever and have faith that if they continue to live as they should, they will all be together again.

In contrast I see the other family, filled with bitterness and frustration, working to get closure or peace through punitive means and the award of money. In comparison, their faith was shallow; they essentially forgot God and relied on worldly remedies for answers. Even though they received a financial settlement, they remained captive to the feelings of anger, resentment, and entitlement that dictated their actions.

The Browns could have been in a courtroom, or an attorney's office, or giving a deposition, or yelling at those who made that fatal mistake. Instead, they were clothing their daughter in sacred, meaningful ways and receiving God's assurance that His hand was over all of them, including Chelsie.

The Brown family went to the temple, cast their burdens on the Lord, did His will, and received His peace. The other family went to the courthouse, cast their burdens on men and worldly solutions, and are still seeking peace.

We all become involved in situations in which mistakes are made and harm is done. We must make choices. Will we trust the Lord and follow Him and His plan, which brings peace now and forever? Or will we look to the world and men's wisdom to give us "justice" and peace—which are beyond their ability to provide? Bickering, bitterness, and searching for justice in worldly ways cannot bring lasting peace, for our Savior is the Prince of Peace and has made it clear: "He that hath the spirit of contention is not of me" (3 Nephi 11:29).

It may seem natural to seek for what we feel is "fair" when we have been wronged. There is a place for attorneys and the court system, and when used properly, they can do much good. We must always remember, however, that God is the only truly just being. He is the only one who understands everything. To receive peace, we must always stay close to Him, as the Browns have so beautifully demonstrated.

Throughout life we all face various situations in which we must decide: Do we choose God and His temple, or the world and its enticements (money, power, fame, etc.). If we go down the world's path, the road back to true peace becomes more difficult to find. Lasting peace comes not from the slippery riches of the world but only from the Prince of Peace—who is always found in His peaceful home, the holy temple. There we can grow in understanding of why we are here, what we are to do here, and what will happen to us when we leave. When we have this eternal perspective, we can always be at peace, even through the storms of this life.

As President Thomas S. Monson reminds us, "Death lays its heavy hand upon those dear to us and at times leaves us baffled and wondering." He noted, "I can think of no greater incentive to inspire compliance with God's commandments and entry to His holy house than the beckoning love of those who have gone ahead and plead for us to follow."[3]

I will not forget the peace, faith, and fulfillment I saw radiating from the faces of the Brown family that early morning in the temple. Nor will I forget the words of their precious Chelsie as she lay dying: "Dad, I want you to cuss them out good—help shake them up to make sure they are more responsible. And then let's be like the Amish and forgive them. It was an accident. I am all right. Make sure you all remain faithful."

Chapter 25

THANKS FOR THE RAINBOWS

An ordinance worker expressed concern for a sister who seemed to be having a difficult time and asked if I would go to the celestial room to see if I could help her. It was late in the afternoon, and as I entered, I was struck by the beauty and peace of the light that filled the room. I looked around for any disturbance but sensed none. A worker whispered that the lady in the far corner had been very tearful a while ago but was more composed now.

I walked over to where she was sitting. She appeared to be at peace and in deep contemplation, so I decided not to disturb her. But as I started to leave, she looked up. I noticed remnants of tears in her eyes, a slight tremor in her clasped hands, but I sensed calmness and hope in her demeanor. I asked if there was anything I could do to help.

She whispered, "Thank you for coming, and thank you for asking. I am fine." She shifted her eyes and gazed intently at the opposite wall. "Thanks for the rainbows. I have been watching their delicate colors and shades." I looked up and over and saw that the sunlight streaming through the windows was being refracted by the crystals in the chandelier, and the entire eastern wall was covered with magnificent rainbows.

She continued in a soft voice, "For a long time I have felt that my trials and troubles would never end. Rain and storms kept coming into my life. I felt as though I were drowning in a sea of unending turmoil and didn't know what to do, but I knew I needed the Lord's help. This morning as I prayed, I had the feeling that there was no better place to receive His help than in His house, so I came.

"I know there is joy in serving others, so during the session, I concentrated intently on the woman I was representing and realized she could not move forward until I opened the door for her. I sensed she was anxious to go through that door. Her readiness and desire to move forward filled my heart with gratitude for the privilege of helping her. I could see that no matter how deep my troubles were, others have carried heavier burdens. As I sensed this, my own troubles seemed to move aside, and my heart was at peace.

"When the session ended, I sat here with closed eyes and felt someone say, 'Thank you.' Warmth filled my soul, and I wanted that feeling to last forever. But soon my own troubles returned to my mind, and I started to sink into the waters of self-pity. No matter how hard I tried to stop these feelings, I felt the storm coming again. I prayed for more faith and asked for the rain to stop. Suddenly an impression came: 'Open your eyes and look.' I opened my eyes and saw that whole wall filled with rainbows. I gasped as I began to absorb the endless beauty of those magnificent colors.

"The promise the Lord gave to Noah millennia ago came to my mind, and I felt He was giving me the same promise:

Remember the rainbow. It is my sign to you and to all

mankind that I am in my heaven and know who you are. I am aware of your challenges. Be faithful. I will carry you safely through the storms so you will not drown in the waters of your troubles. Little by little they will recede, and you will understand my unending love for you and for all mankind. The rainbow will give you hope. Be faithful and all will be well (see Genesis 9:13–17).

She looked directly at me and said, "I know I will not drown. I know the rain will stop, and the waters will recede. I know I will be all right. You have other things to do. Don't worry about me. Thanks again for the rainbows."

The radiance of her face, the sureness of her words, and the strength of her testimony seemed to meld seamlessly into the beautiful rainbows shimmering throughout the room, and I could say no more. I turned and slowly left the room with my eyes fastened on the soft colors moving higher on the eastern wall as the sun moved lower in the western sky.

The depth of beauty and understanding the light and crystals gave to that celestial setting brought tears of gratitude to my eyes. I knew that faithful sister, and all others like her, would be all right. She had seen the rainbows, understood God's covenants, and received the assurance of His help, light, and love—the eternal source of all lasting peace.

I returned to my office and went about my duties with a lighter step, a quieter voice, and a greater sense of gratitude. I was more certain than ever that temples are where heaven and earth connect, with each connection suited to the specific need of those who humbly seek Him. Everyone will have burdens to carry and storms to weather; some may even feel they are drowning in the waters of those storms. But God has covenanted with us that as we serve Him by serving others, the Savior will safely support us through every storm, for He has carried *all* these burdens and weathered *every* storm.

God wants us to remember the covenants He made with our fathers Adam, Noah, Abraham, and many others. We sometimes call these covenants ancient, but since they are eternal and extend through all generations, they are as new, as meaningful, and as powerful today as they were when they were originally given.

Throughout the ages, God has given signs and tokens to His children—signs such as rainbows—to remind us of His covenants and His love. Temples and covenants go hand in hand. What a blessing temples are in allowing us to make, renew, remember, contemplate, and keep these covenants. As we understand and gain our own testimony of these covenants, they become operative in our lives and, just as this good woman did, we receive the needed strength from them to carry on.

Every time I enter a celestial room, I close my eyes, see a wall full of celestial color, and hear a humble sister gazing heavenward and quietly saying, "Thanks for the rainbows."

Chapter 26

I STILL DON'T GET IT

One evening I noticed a young man pacing back and forth in the foyer of the temple. I thanked him for coming and asked if there was anything I could do to help. With a playful smile he responded, "Just tell my wife to hurry up." He said his name was Bob, and we visited for a few moments. He had an engaging personality and an aura of honesty about him that you couldn't help but warm to. Soon he spotted his wife, took her case from her, and introduced me to Mary. I felt a spirit of goodness and patience about her. Bob was anxious to leave, so they quickly departed.

I occasionally noticed Bob in the late evening patiently (and sometimes not so patiently) waiting for his wife. We often visited for a few moments and after a few months became somewhat acquainted. Bob always seemed to be in a hurry to leave as soon as Mary appeared, so I never really got acquainted with her. During one of our visits, Bob mentioned that they had four children ranging in age from twelve to five and that it was Mary's idea to come to the temple regularly.

One evening Bob asked if we could visit for a moment in my office. He was sure his wife would be a while, and he could see the foyer through the open door of my office. "May I tell you a little about our family and then ask you a question?" I nodded, and he proceeded:

"I love my wife and children. I grew up in the Church but did not serve a mission. My wife and I were married civilly, but a few years later we were sealed in the temple. I try to be a good husband and father, but sometimes I wonder if I really am. My wife loves the temple and wants me to come with her. I want to make her happy so I come, but truthfully, I don't have the same enthusiasm for the temple she does. Don't get me wrong, I feel good when we come, but so far I just don't seem to 'get it' like she does.

"My question is this: What's the difference? Why does Mary seem so fulfilled and excited about the temple, and I don't? What is it that she 'gets' that I don't?"

I appreciated his honesty and sincerity and explained that we all learn at different rates. I told him that over time the Lord would give him a deeper understanding and love for the temple. I commended him for his sincere desire to bless his wife and children and assured him the Lord would bless him. Just then he noticed Mary entering the foyer and quickly left with a final comment: "Maybe we can talk more another time. And, please, don't tell her about our visit. See you."

I was intrigued by his comments and question, and I wanted to help him. I could tell he really wanted to feel better about the temple. I prayed for what to say or do to help him, but the only impression I received was that over time the Lord would bless him with more understanding and joy.

Several weeks later we visited again in my office. I asked if he felt any different. He replied, "Not really." I told him again that I knew the Lord was pleased with him and his desire to be a good father and husband and to make his wife happy. I explained that though I wanted to help him feel the joy and fulfillment from the temple that his wife did, he would have to discover that for himself. I testified that as he continued to attend, joy and understanding would come. He promised he would keep coming and then added:

"I don't believe I have as much faith as my wife does, but I want you to know that I am very grateful for her and her faith. I come mainly because of her and have a good feeling when we are here. I still wonder, however, why I struggle to find the desire to attend the temple."

Without waiting for a response from me he continued, "I'm afraid if it weren't for Mary, I would probably choose something else to do. That isn't really right, is it? Why do you suppose I have this attitude toward something that my wife finds essential to her happiness?"

Without knowing more about his background and experience, all I could do was commend him for his love and faithfulness to his wife and family and assure him that God loved him and would bless him. I encouraged him to increase his prayers of gratitude for his wife, for the temple, for God's help, and to "hang in there." He said he would.

Bob kept coming to the temple with Mary, and he also kept asking me why he didn't feel the same way his wife did. "Why are there so many other things I would rather do? Why don't I 'get it' the way she does?" I kept encouraging him and assuring him that eventually God would give him the understanding and joy he desired. He always expressed appreciation for this encouragement.

Months rolled by, and the time for our release drew near.

With so many things to do and so little time, we were bus-ier than ever. We loved serving in the temple and everyone there and wanted to express our love for them over and over again.

With just a few days left, I noticed Bob in the foyer one evening. There were several groups of people coming and go-ing, so we didn't visit much, but I did ask him how things were. With a twinkle in his eye, he shrugged his shoulders and replied, "It's about the same. We keep coming. I keep feeling good about it. I love my wife and children. Don't worry, I'll keep coming. I know it is right. I'm sorry that I still don't 'get it'—at least not like Mary does or the way I'd like to. Anyway, thanks for your help and encouragement. I promise I'll hang in there."

I moved among the crowd, expressing my love and ap-preciation to as many as I could. I felt as though I were in heaven as I mingled with those wonderful, faithful people. A little later, Bob and Mary came over and thanked us for our service and wished me well. What radiant smiles they had! My emotions were already close to the surface, but see-ing their warm, loving smiles and feeling their goodness and faithfulness almost brought me to tears, especially as I real-ized I might not see them again. I wondered if I had helped them as much as I should have.

When the foyer emptied, I went to my office and began thinking about all of the things we needed to finish before we would leave that special place. Bob and Mary kept com-ing to my mind. I wished I could have done more to help them and began to worry a little about their future. What would happen? Would they keep coming? Would Bob finally "get it"?

As I thought of this I heard in my mind the following—not as a rebuke, but as a reminder: This is my temple. This is my work; you are given the opportunity to help. Bob is my son; Mary is my daughter. I love them. You can and should love them and help them in every way you can, but remember, they are in my hands—as are you. You have done what you could, and I am pleased. Keep trying. I will do the rest. Continue faithful.

I sat musing on this when suddenly I seemed to be transported to a different sphere. Everything was beautiful and peaceful. I was surrounded by happy people, much as I had been in the temple foyer earlier that evening. I felt no rush to get things done but rather to express love and gratitude and help in any way I could. Everyone was filled with light and love and goodness, and I knew I was among friends.

Suddenly the crowd stood still and from somewhere, and maybe from everywhere, I heard the question:

"Lord, when saw we thee an hungred, and fed thee? or thirsty, and gave thee drink? When saw we thee a stranger, and took thee in? or naked, and clothed thee? Or when saw we thee sick, or in prison, and came unto thee?" (Matthew 25:37–39).

Then a loving reply:

"Verily I say unto you, Inasmuch as ye have done it unto one of the least of these my brethren, ye have done it unto me" (Matthew 25:40).

I looked around and saw Bob in the crowd. He had a look of wonder on his face and said, "Really? I thought I was just being good to my wife. Those men I represented were really let out of prison? They were actually clothed with the priesthood? They were taught and fed the bread and water of life and made whole because of something I did? Really? That's great! Thanks for allowing me to help. I always felt good and kept coming but never realized it would end up like this. Thanks so much! I finally *get it*." His eyes were twinkling, his smile was broader than ever, and his whole being was aglow. He turned, reached for the hand of his beloved Mary, and together they quietly moved from my view.

My eyes were foggy and my throat full as I continued to hear more:

"Because thou hast seen me, thou hast believed; blessed are they that have not seen, and yet have believed" (John 20:29).

"Blessed are ye if ye shall believe in me . . . after that ye have seen me and know that I am. And again, more blessed are they who shall believe in your words" (3 Nephi 12:1–2).

"To others it is given to believe on their words, that they also might have eternal life if they continue faithful" (D&C 46:14).

I knew that Bob and Mary had continued faithful. I felt God's deep love for them and sensed His special tenderness for those who, like Bob, don't seem to quite get it but continue faithful anyway. There was more, but suffice it to say that before I left that special place, I understood that all who, like Bob, continue faithful would not only eventually get it but ultimately would get it all.

Chapter 27

PEACE

I was walking across the foyer of the temple to an appointment when a young couple asked if they could speak to me for a moment. They expressed their love for the temple and with stars in their eyes said, "We were married here a few weeks ago and have returned regularly. We want you to know that with the strength we receive from the temple we feel we can take on the whole world and do whatever the Lord asks of us."

For a second I was tempted to temper their youthful exuberance a bit, but upon sensing their confidence and feeling their faith, I instead gave them a hug of encouragement and assured them that indeed they could accomplish whatever God asked of them. They smiled and, arm in arm, confidently opened the door to the outside world and disappeared from my view. Instinctively I said to myself, There they go, just like Adam and Eve, leaving the comfort and security of God's home, striking out on their own into the unknown world, filled with the assurance that as they call upon God, He will bless and guide them in every needful way.

I was so caught up in those feelings that I hardly felt

Courtesy Intellectual Reserve, Inc.

With faith, courage, and hope, Adam and Eve go forth from the garden.

the touch as someone said, "Oh, sorry—sometimes my cane gets ahead of me." I now saw an older, somewhat crippled gentleman making his way towards the door. I walked with him, and as I opened the door for him, he turned his head so he could see me and said, "I love being in the temple. It's a wonderful place and a wonderful work. While I'm here helping others, my pain and loneliness cease to exist. Give my gratitude to all the workers. I love it here."

As he shuffled out the door I seemed to see ancient Simeon who, after thanking God for the privilege of seeing the infant Jesus and the coming of "thy salvation," whispered, "Lord, now lettest thou thy servant depart in peace, according to thy word" (Luke 2:29; see vv. 25–35). Beautiful sensations filled my heart as I contemplated all who over time and space have loved, served, and found peace in temples.

I was still lost in these feelings when a gentle tug on my arm brought me back to the foyer. As I turned I saw an older, widowed ordinance worker smiling in understanding. "With the strength I receive from the temple," she whispered, "I also am sure I can make it to the end of whatever time the Lord has in mind for me." I knew this good woman was in the temple often and told her I too was certain she could and would make it faithfully to the end. She turned to go, and I seemed to see faithful Anna who was in the temple often and who gave thanks for the privilege of seeing Mary and Joseph and the baby Jesus and understanding the redemption He would bring (see Luke 2:38).

Visions of faithful people serving in temples from the beginning of time filled my heart and soul. It was clear that what these latter-day faithful people were experiencing that day had been experienced many times before and would continue to be experienced over and over again forever.

Suddenly I remembered my appointment and hurried off, arriving just in time. When I finished, I started back across the foyer to my office when a middle-aged couple greeted me and asked if we could visit for a moment. They started by expressing their love for the temple and the peace it brought to them and then told of a son who was going down a path that was bringing them and others great pain. They thought they had taught him properly, but despite their efforts and faith and prayers, he seemed to be going deeper into the dark. Without asking why or seeking consolation, they said, "We feel the best thing we can do right now is come to the temple more often. The light, love, and promise of the temple strengthen our determination to keep trying and never give up. What a blessing the 'foreverness' of the temple is to us. Though we feel pain, we also feel joy in the promise that as we stay faithful, things will somehow work out."

They thanked me for listening, and as they turned and

left, it was as though I were seeing Alma and his good wife praying in faith for their own wayward son. Somehow I knew that a temple was involved there also. How many times had this story repeated itself, and how many times would it be repeated? As I contemplated their love, their faithfulness, and their desire to obey God and bless others, I knew that things would somehow work out for these concerned parents and their wayward son also. I didn't know how or when, just that they would.

I entered my office, and as soon as I sat down at my desk, my mind filled with thoughts and feelings of other people from the scriptures, as well as people today, being blessed in so many ways by the temple. I recalled an experience from the first day the temple in Tonga was open for ordinance work. It was a hugely busy day, as dozens of happy couples and families came to be sealed. When the day drew to a close and just a few people were left, Jean and I felt impressed to leave and let others finish up. Outside we noticed seven, well-dressed children sitting quietly under a tree. We asked if they were waiting for someone, and they replied that they were waiting to be sealed to their parents. (There was not a youth center in the temple at that time.) I asked their names and how long they had been waiting. They introduced themselves and said they had been waiting since early morning. I asked if they had eaten lunch, and they replied that they weren't hungry.

I went back into the temple and saw a couple patiently waiting on a bench. I asked their name, and sure enough, it was the same as the children's. I asked if they had turned in their paper work. "Yes—early this morning," was their reply. "We are waiting to be called for our sealing."

Concerned that they had been overlooked, I went to the recorders' area, and we began looking through the large stack of forms. Partway through, there it was! It had become clipped to the papers before it and had not been processed, so through the day this couple (and their children) waited and waited and waited. It was the first experience for this family with the temple, and the thought of asking how long it might take or to question anything else never entered their minds. After all, they knew they were in the Lord's house and trusted He would take care of all that needed to be done.

Admiring their great faith and patience, I told them it was now their time to be sealed. I asked the ordinance workers and sealers not to mention the error but let the Spirit of the Lord do the explaining and the blessing. The children were gathered, the sealing took place, and the Spirit of the Lord descended in such rich abundance that it mattered not whether they had waited for hours or days or years—they were now an eternal family!

After I finished reliving that experience, I was taken to another setting where I seemed to see many other families in tents facing a temple. They were all patiently and faithfully listening to their prophet-king as he explained many important principles about the Savior and eternal truth. I saw their hearts open and their faith increase as they fell to the earth crying for forgiveness. Then I saw them filled with the same joy I had witnessed in some of their descendants in Tonga (see Mosiah 2–4). Oh, how the love and blessings from the temple are needed by all—over all time and in all places!

In my mind's eye, suddenly I was on the open deck of a large ship plowing its way towards New Zealand with over a hundred Tongan Saints aboard—again, modern-day

Courtesy Intellectual Reserve, Inc.

King Benjamin Addresses His People, *by Gary L. Kapp.*

descendants of those listening from their tents. I felt the choppy seas and saw many seasick children being comforted by their parents, huddled together, singing the songs of Zion and visiting reverently about the temple blessings they were anticipating. I noticed the Loni Sikahema family, and for some reason focused on little five-year-old Vai. As I reflected on the faithfulness of the Sikahema family and others similar to them, I was reminded anew of the eternal blessings the temple brings to those who participate in holy ordinances and make and keep sacred covenants, regardless of the sacrifices involved.

My mind then moved to Argentina, where I saw a particular family from one of the indigenous groups of Paraguay. They had traveled for many difficult days to be sealed for eternity in the Buenos Aires Argentina Temple. The parents, teenagers, children, and infant were all dressed in white, all glowing—each with the assurance in their countenance that if they remained faithful, they would be together forever. I

saw one little cherubic face most clearly. Then I remembered
the day we received word that while on their way home from
the temple, traveling on foot in a hot, humid area, that precious infant had succumbed to what, they knew not—only
that he was gone. Because they were in a remote area, they
had of necessity buried him by the side of the rugged trail
and moved on.

I saw again that cherubic smile and watched the glisten-
ing eyes of the parents as they explained, "He is gone but not
really, for he is ours forever. We will live for him." Oh, the
comfort, peace, and assurance temples give!

I thought of the Mormon pioneers crossing the plains and
their faith as they buried loved ones along the way. I knew
that the temple had prepared and strengthened both them
and these more recent-day Saints from Paraguay for what lay
ahead. From eternity to eternity the temple has helped and
strengthened and will continue to help and strengthen all
who rely thereon—including you and me—forever.

My thoughts then took me to Mongolia, where I watched
a colorfully dressed family leave their beloved steppes and
sheep and wend their way by horse and cart and bus and
plane through confusing traffic, the hassle of border regula-
tions and intimidating passport desks, and the discomfort of
constraining seat belts, traveling through and above banks
of towering clouds and threatening storms, to finally arrive
at the temple in Hong Kong. Remembering this determined
family for some reason reminded me of Shadrach, Meshach
and Abed-nego and their great faith as consuming fires of
change raged around them but scorched them not. Someway,
the believing blood of Israel had found its way into these

faithful nomadic people in a remote place on the earth and drew them to the temple.

After their sealing had taken place, I asked this remarkable family if they would sing "I Am a Child of God" to a group of Church leaders from throughout Asia who happened to be gathered in Hong Kong at that time. The family was rather shy and unsure about many things, but they were completely sure about the sealing they had experienced in the temple and did not hesitate to enthusiastically sing, in their Mongolian tongue, "I Am a Child of God." Everyone blessed to hear them knew that the Lord had successfully guided latter-day hunters and fishers in gathering some of scattered Israel to the temple (see Jeremiah 16:16).

Those who a hundred and fifty years earlier had traveled by ship across broad oceans or by handcart or wagon or on foot across vast deserts to come to Zion have no more claim on faithfulness than these modern-day Mongolian pioneers. Their faith in Jesus Christ and their testimony of Him, possessed by all of these Saints, nurtured their desire to get to the temple and emboldened and strengthened them to do things they otherwise could not have done.

I next found myself on a beautiful hill in Rexburg, Idaho. I had been assigned, as a member of the Presidency of the Seventy, to dedicate the ground for the construction of the temple there. We were asked to mention the event only to the stakes in the new Rexburg temple district and not look for a big crowd. But I had worked with and known the wonderful people of that area, including the BYU–Idaho students, long enough to know that all who could come would come.

The date set was a time when school was not in session,

yet on the morning of the dedication, here they came, and came, and came—up the hills, over the fields, from everywhere. When we began, more than seven thousand of the best people in the world were reverently and patiently waiting to participate in that momentous event.

I looked into the sparkling faces of thousands of young men and young women and felt their love and gratitude for the promise of this new temple. They were eager to follow their leaders and to be of even greater service and to help in any way they could.

As I studied these representatives of the rising generation, suddenly I seemed to see another gathering of thousands of sparkling young men, supported and encouraged by an equal number of beautiful young women. I felt their faith and the faith of all those about them as that group of "stripling" warriors eagerly flocked together to follow their leaders (Alma 53:22). They were going off to war with swords and shields of steel, but even more important, they had the "sword of the Spirit," the "shield of faith," and the "breastplate of righteousness" (Ephesians 6:14–17). Their assignment: Protect and save a nation.

I looked again at those sitting in front of me and realized that nearly all of them either had served or soon would serve missions where they would follow their leaders and fight darkness and evil wherever and however assigned. Though their battles would be fought in a different way from that of the two thousand stripling warriors, those battles would be as difficult and as critical. Like the stripling warriors, the missionaries would be armed with the sword of the spirit, the shield of faith, and the breastplate of righteousness. They would not fear because they had been taught well by their

It's True, Sir—All Present and Accounted For, *by Clark Kelley Price.*

mothers and fathers. I knew they would serve admirably and be protected miraculously, just like their earlier counterparts, as they filled their roles in proclaiming and protecting the truth and building the kingdom of God (see Alma 53:16–22; 56:47–48).

As the services began and everyone started singing, my eyes were opened even wider, and I seemed to see countless other groups of young people coming from everywhere—up hills, through valleys, across oceans, even it seemed from beyond mortal bounds—coming to temples, receiving strength and power from on high, and going forth to serve, to protect, and to save.

As I saw them return with honor, I caught a glimpse of joyful embraces, shared excitement, and warm embraces from grateful parents, family members, sweethearts, and the Lord Himself. It was sweet beyond measure.

My mind next went to a winter day in the beautifully refurbished Idaho Falls Visitors' Center by the temple. A class of somewhat rowdy Primary children had just entered, taken off their coats, and assembled around the impressive Christus statue. The giggles, chatter, and pushing gradually subsided as they sat down to listen to their teacher. When the guide pushed a button, a soft yet penetrating voice representing the Savior filled the area. "I am Jesus Christ . . ." There was total silence from the young folks, and I saw a look of awe in their eyes. One seven-year-old boy turned to his friend and said, "Jesus is talking to me."

That precious group then moved reverently to the picture window. As they took in the breathtaking view of the temple, I heard one young girl whisper, "I'm going to get married there someday. The angel just invited me and said he would wait for me."

Observing the wonder experienced by these precious children, I found myself in the ancient city of Bountiful, seeing the same looks of awe and reverence on the faces of children as they gazed at the temple and listened to the voice of the resurrected Savior. The faces were so real and the feelings so powerful that I was overcome with gratitude and wonder. I seemed to see everyone—past, present, and future—moving towards the temple—towards the Savior. The temple always has been and always will be the ultimate focal point in our coming unto the Savior. Our progress or lack thereof is inexorably tied to the covenants of the temple, obedience to which opens the windows of heaven and pours out blessings beyond compare. Suddenly I heard endless streams of faithful people singing: "Glory, and honor, and power, and might, be ascribed to our God; for he is full of mercy, justice, grace and truth, and peace, forever and ever, Amen" (D&C 84:102).

I saw the faces of many people, some mentioned in the scriptures, some not, but all full of hope, looking to their posterity and praying that they would also treasure their

Courtesy Intellectual Reserve, Inc.

Christ and Children from around the World,
by Del Parson.

covenants. Then I saw the faces of many people today following the examples set by their forebears and realized that down the stream of time the thing that will be of most worth to everyone will be our honoring, even our treasuring, our temple covenants—individually and as families. As we treasure our covenants, they become an eternal treasure to us, to our ancestors, and to our posterity. Most of our other accomplishments will fade away, but whether consciously or unconsciously, past and future members of our families, on both sides of the veil, will look with praise on our having treasured our temple covenants, of which they are such an important part—and believe me, they will know.

You don't have to be some famous missionary or have

held so-called high callings to be among the throng of the noble. You just need to go regularly to the temple, make and keep sacred covenants, and above all, treasure them! By truly treasuring our temple covenants, every good thing is tied together, bound and sealed, never to be broken.

As these truths filled every fiber of my being, I found myself physically exhausted yet spiritually exhilarated and wanting to understand more. I could sense, however, that this particular set of experiences—or "visions," if you will—was coming to a close. As I returned to my office in the temple, I felt impressed to open the scriptures and read: "Verily I say unto you, all . . . who know their hearts are honest and are broken, and their spirits contrite, and are willing to observe their covenants by sacrifice . . . are accepted of me. For I, the Lord, will cause them to bring forth as a very fruitful tree which is planted in a goodly land, by a pure stream, that yieldeth much precious fruit" (D&C 97:8–9).

Whether it be the example of Adam and Eve, of Simeon and Anna, of Alma and his wife, of the stripling warriors and their mothers, fathers, brothers and sisters, and girlfriends, or the shining countenances of children reflecting the love of the Savior, or of your own sacred diligence—the temple is the key.

President Thomas S. Monson has promised: "As you and I go to the holy houses of God, as we remember the covenants we make within, we will be more able to bear every trial and to overcome each temptation. In this sacred sanctuary we will find peace; we will be renewed and fortified."[1]

Oh, to treasure our temple covenants forever, that we might one day hear the Savior say: "These things I have spoken unto you, that in me ye might have peace" (John 16:33).

Chapter 28

IT'S ALL THERE

I felt an unusually strong spirit of goodness coming from the one hundred-plus ordinance workers who had gathered for an early morning joint instruction meeting. Each seemed alert, and all were eager for the instruction they would receive so they could better serve in the temple that day.

During the opening hymn, one of the coordinators leaned over and whispered, "They are all here—no exceptions—everyone in his or her place."

"Everyone?" I questioned.

"Yes. Everyone!"

A warm feeling of gratitude filled my soul. Everyone here! Amazing! I studied the faces before me and thought of the challenges they had overcome to be here, yet everyone was here—physically, mentally, emotionally, and spiritually! My heart swelled, and I received an impression that God had something important to say to them. I was not sure what it was, but I knew He would reveal it when the time was right.

As I finished the scheduled training, I felt impressed to share something President David O. McKay had said many years before about the temple. In a meeting with some

General Authorities, President McKay, who had just come from a session in the temple, said, "Brethren, I think I am finally beginning to understand."[1]

Here was the president of the Church, who had been going to the temple regularly for more than sixty years, humbly acknowledging that after his lifetime of service, he was just *beginning* to understand the temple ceremonies and ordinances, and though he knew much, he still had more to learn.

I told the temple workers that in 1954, just a few weeks after I had arrived in the mission field, President McKay visited Tonga as part of his worldwide tour. He spoke to the missionaries and bore his testimony of the Savior and challenged all of us to be good missionaries. I was one of about fifteen sitting on the floor in front of him. His piercing eyes seemed to look right through my soul, and I knew he was a prophet, that the Savior lived, and that I must be a good missionary.

As the power of testimony filled the room, the words of the shift coordinator, *They are all here!* returned to my mind, and I said, "Brothers and Sisters, I want you to know that just as you are all here, so the truths of eternity are all here! We may not yet understand them all, but they are all here. As you, along with your father Abraham, have a desire to 'possess a greater knowledge' (Abraham 1:2) and as you listen to the whisperings of the Spirit, you will gain that greater knowledge 'line upon line, precept upon precept, here a little and there a little' (2 Nephi 28:10)."

Eternal truths and understanding flowed through my mind. I told the workers that since God knows everything, and since the temple ceremonies and ordinances come

*Church President David O. McKay with mission president D'Monte Coombs
(left) and Elder John H. Groberg (right) in Tonga, January 1955.*

from Him, there is no end to what we can learn from them.
President McKay knew the Savior. He also understood the
temple well but knew he must continue to learn more. I
promised the workers that as they continued to serve with
pure hearts they, along with President McKay, would be able
to say with surety that they know the Savior lives, that the
temple is His home, and that they are "beginning to understand." I testified that over time they would understand more
and more, until they would eventually partake fully of the
Lord's promise: "That which is of God is light; and he that
receiveth light, and continueth in God, receiveth more light;

and that light groweth brighter and brighter until the perfect day" (D&C 50:24).

I closed by testifying again that since the Savior lives, and since the fulness of truth is in Him, and since He is in His temple—*It is all here*. The workers nodded in agreement and reverently went to their assignments. The glow coming from them testified that they were filled with righteous desire and wanted to help the Lord in every way they could to bless all who entered His house that day, from either side of the veil.

I attended an endowment session during that shift and was deeply impressed by the intricacy and variety of all that was said and done in the presentation of the plan of salvation. Everything was in such perfect order and blended into such a beautiful tapestry of eternal goodness and light and truth that it seemed almost beyond human comprehension. At times I caught glimpses of such deep and endless meanings that I knew these truths could only come from the Spirit and be discerned by the Spirit. After the session I went to my office to be alone for a while.

As I contemplated all I had heard, seen, and felt, an experience I had had as a young missionary began to fill my mind and soul. The memory of that experience became so vivid, it was as though I were back in Tonga, reliving that event.

Five of us had been away preaching on several small islands for many days and were returning home in a small sailboat. We had hoped to be home that evening, but the wind turned contrary, the seas became rough, and it was obvious we would be on the ocean the rest of that day and probably that night and into the next day. It did no good to complain, so I accepted the situation for what it was and prayed that we might reach home safely. We were jolted and slapped by steel waves, and as darkness fell the temperature fell also. I tried to sleep but couldn't. We took turns visiting with the boat's captain, trying to help him in any way we could.

After much of the night had passed, I noticed that the captain was alone, so I went to his side. He was holding the sail rope with one hand, the rudder pole with the other. He was alert and paying close attention to everything around him. A slight shudder went through me as I realized how literally we were trusting our lives to the skill and goodness of this older gentleman! As I sensed his deep concentration and determination to get us home safely, a feeling of love and gratitude washed over me.

We visited, and he told me of his faith in God and of his certainty that his experience and skill came from God. He said he knew God was the Creator of the whole universe, including the stormy sea we were currently on. Our conversation was often interrupted by large waves or strong gusts of wind that whipped the sail and tipped us precariously close to the water. The captain, however, always maintained control. I asked what I could do to help during his long, lonely vigil. He said he was fine but appreciated the company, so we continued to visit. After one lengthy bout of moving back and forth between dark waves I asked, "Do you know where we are?" He smiled and nodded, so I asked, "And just where are we?"

When a calmer moment came he asked me to hold the sail rope. He kept one hand on the rudder, lay back, and dropped his free arm into the ocean. He looked searchingly into the heavens, concentrated deeply, and was silent for a long time.

Finally everything seemed to click into place, and he sat up, pointed to the horizon, and said, "In a short while, the sun will rise right there. When it does, the island of Lofanga will be over there, the island of Nukupule over there, and the island of Lifuka straight ahead. We will have gone around the outer reef and will be close to entering the calm waters of Pangai Harbor." He spoke so confidently that it was easy to believe him. He took the sail rope back, and we continued on.

Before long I noticed a speck of light on the dark horizon. It got brighter and brighter, and suddenly the sun peeked over the horizon and sent a path of light shimmering across the sea, warming and welcoming us into its embrace. Soon we could make out a few landmarks, and sure enough, everything was just as the captain had said: Lofanga was over there, Nukupule was over there, the deadly reef was behind us, and we were moving directly toward the calm waters of Pangai Harbor.

Even though I had believed the captain, I was still amazed at how accurate his sense of direction had been. I asked if he would explain how he avoided the reef and knew where the other islands were and where the harbor was. He said that when he put his arm in the water he could feel the difference in the warmth, speed, and direction of the currents, which helped him determine how close the islands or reefs were. When he listened to the wind and the waves, he understood many things from the volume and direction of various sounds. Pointing to the sky, he said that even though it was stormy and cloudy, he could see a few stars here and there and even an occasional bird that flitted in and out of the clouds. All of this helped him accurately calculate our position.

He went on to explain other things, which I did not understand, but I knew he did. I listened with awe and reverence and marveled at his exquisite mind and astonishing ability. He had known not only where we were but what he needed to do to bring us safely home. A thrill of wonder passed through me just from being in the presence of such a brilliant and yet humble, confident soul. He had no compass, no radio, no mechanical help, but he had his mind, his body, his experience, and above all, his faith in God. The combination of all these was bringing us safely home.

As the boat moved steadily toward the harbor, a quiet peace settled over me, and a parallel truth came to my heart. Just as I had, with trust and confidence, willingly put my life into the hands of a skilled and experienced Tongan sea captain to carry me safely home, I could with trust and confidence put my life into the hands of Jesus, my skilled and experienced celestial Captain, trusting full well that He would carry me safely to my heavenly home. Though there would be stormy seas and treacherous shoals in this life and unfathomable complexities in the universe beyond, yet He would bring me and all who trust Him safely home to Zion's peaceful harbor.

As we left the rough seas and entered the calmer waters of the harbor, someone offered a vocal prayer of gratitude, and we sang hymns of praise—as we always did upon approaching home.[2]

As we sang, I understood why so many of the early Christian hymns express gratitude for reaching safe harbor.

Detail from a painting by Clark Kelley Price

Those pilgrims actually experienced, as I had, the fury and the monotony of travel by sail. They knew what it was like to be buffeted by the wind and the waves, they knew in whom they trusted, and they knew the joy of safe arrival. Today we travel smoothly and rapidly by car or airplane and too often take safe arrivals for granted, thus missing the overwhelming feeling of gratitude others have experienced. I hoped I would always be grateful for safe arrivals.

As we moved alongside the wharf, ropes were tossed and secured. We gathered our belongings and prepared to go ashore. I thanked the captain for bringing us home safely and expressed my love and admiration for him. He nodded shyly, but I could tell he also was very grateful for this safe arrival. I threw my belongings over my shoulder, climbed onto the wharf, and looked back at the captain. He was busy bailing out bilge water, cleaning the boat, and getting ready for his next voyage.

As I watched him work, I felt a renewed sense of gratitude

and love for this quiet, skillful Tongan captain. We made eye contact, and both of us nodded in acknowledgment of God's goodness.

As I thought of this, I felt another set of eyes and was filled with gratitude and love for our eternal Captain, Jesus Christ. It was as though I could see Him and His co-workers carrying people safely home and then turning around, going back into the deep, and bringing others safely home. Though I was physically weak, I felt a surge of spiritual strength and sensed that these feelings were being indelibly etched into my mind and soul.

These are the memories that flooded my mind as I sat in my office in the temple. The experience had been so real it was as though I was actually reliving that voyage of decades before. I was seeing eyes and remembering feelings as clearly as the day they happened! I saw the captain's hands and eyes and ears and felt his mind measuring everything and doing whatever was needed to bring us safely home. I saw President McKay's piercing eyes and beckoning hands and felt his certain testimony as he encouraged us to be good missionaries. I saw our eternal Captain's eyes and hands and felt His strength, love, and desire to bring us safely home.

New vistas of understanding opened to my mind, and I found myself repeating the words: "It's all there. It's all here." These memories were like a photograph or a masterful painting—everything is already there, but each time we study the photo or painting more carefully and in better light, we see things we had not seen before. I now saw that in the same way it takes the proper functioning of each part of the temple to make it complete, it takes the proper functioning of each part of our body to make it complete, and it takes the proper orbiting of each star in the universe to make it complete and bring balance and order to everything else.

I understood that it is only through the power of the Spirit that our temples, our bodies, and the whole universe function properly and stay alive. I understood that all orders of orbits—whether stars in the universe, tides on this earth, or internal systems within our bodies—are inexorably linked together. I perceived that size and distance and location and speed are not the determining factors, but attunement with the Spirit is. Proper yielding and humble submission or adjustment (which is really faith in the Lord Jesus Christ and sincere repentance) are the keys to becoming part of that great eternal round that contains all truth and to receiving strength and understanding from it (see D&C 3:2; 1 Nephi 10:19; Alma 7:20; 37:12; Abraham 3). This is something that all the prophets have understood, and when we are fully in tune with all of this, we will have eternal life.

I seemed to see countless orbits, not only of stars and planets and suns and systems of incomprehensible magnitude but of the whirling systems within each cell of our bodies and minds, all moving in perfect order and following a celestial cadence. I saw my Tongan captain linking facts and feelings together, as his spirit and mind were energized and expanded by the power of his faith in Christ. In a miraculous way, he was actually attuning all these orbits, both from within and without, to the eternal synchronized humming of the universe, which triggered within him slight movements or adjustments (similar to repentance), which caused our craft to go around dangerous reefs and hidden shoals and move inexorably forward along the course that would take us safely home.

In a similar manner, through the workings of the Holy Ghost, we can get our bearings from the orbits of the stars, currents, sounds, and feelings, both within and without. Thus through faith in Christ, we can attune our spirits to the innumerable orbits within each cell of our body, as well as those from the universe beyond and receive understanding of where we are and what adjustments (repentance) we need to make to arrive home safely.

In this sense, the atonement of Jesus Christ is an "attunement." When our lives get out of tune with the Lord's Spirit (the truths of eternity), we emit discordant vibes into the universe, which if not repented of or changed, create serious problems by taking us away from the orbit of truth. The Savior atoned for our sins, thus making it possible for Him to attune our lives to the truths of eternity, if we will believe, repent, be baptized, and receive the Holy Ghost. Thus, through time, we can receive strength and understanding from that eternal infinite humming that God has set in motion throughout the universe.

The same is true for our temporal body—our own "temple." If the orbits of the cells within our body get out of tune with each other (through drugs, anger, or other causes), they move in a different course, which is counter to the wholeness of life and to the unity that God created in us. That different course, if not corrected, brings death (physical and/or spiritual).

When Paul explained that "all the building fitly framed together groweth unto an holy temple in the Lord" (Ephesians 2:21), he was trying to help us understand this principle better. The various blessings given and received in the temple make it possible for the faithful to become complete—"fitly framed" or fully attuned. As we listen to every word, of every part, including the initial part, which we sometimes overlook, we can feel what adjustments we need to make. When we make those adjustments, we begin the process of attunement, which over time eventuates in eternal life. As President McKay explained, when our wills and desires coalesce with the Lord's, we begin to understand.

The scriptures and our leaders tell us that we often live far below our privileges—that we have the ability to use God's gifts at a much higher level. We are entitled to personal revelation, which is God's Spirit speaking to our spirit. When we pay closer attention to everything in the temple, everything in our bodies, and everything in the universe, we receive more spiritual attunement and understand that *it's all there*—and can all be ours if we are willing to increase our faith in God and improve our actions.

My Tongan captain had no formal navigational training and was not acquainted with radios, motors, radar, or other modern man-made "miracles." However, he believed in God, knew the sea, was at home with the winds, the waves, the currents, the tides, the reefs, the stars, the sails, and much, much more. He believed that God had placed within him everything he needed in order to bring us to safe harbor, and acting on this faith, he did so.

Similarly, we don't need to be educated in worldly ways to go through the temple and receive its blessings. We just need to believe in God, trust and act on the feelings, promises, and instructions we receive there, and move forward to safe harbor.

All truth, technological or otherwise, comes from God, and He expects us to find and use it. I am grateful for scientific advancements that help us move faster and farther and guide us over endless seas, arid deserts, rugged mountains, and crowded highways. I am beginning to understand, however, that when mortal man reaches the limits of all the education he can conjure up, when he builds the fastest computer he can conceive, when he does all within his mental grasp, he will still fall short of what I witnessed when a humble, believing Tongan captain brought us safely home by melding eternal truths through faith in God into something that surpasses all the technology that mortal man will ever create.

As man discovers more and more truth, he will eventually come full circle and realize that through faith in the Lord Jesus Christ, there is already within each of us the greatest and most complete storehouse of knowledge, truth, and power anywhere. When fully developed, it can move mountains, heal the sick, and organize worlds (see Moses 1:33; 7:13–14; Matthew 8:3).

Yes, it's all there. It's all within us; it's all in the temple; it's all throughout the universe. God put it there. His love fills the whole universe! When we exercise faith in God, we tap into a power that is already there and that allows Him to do what is necessary to bring us safely home. The Savior not only ascended on high but descended below all things and comprehended all things (see D&C 88:6). He has agreed to be our Captain throughout eternity. He can and will help us in any and every situation and will see us through to eternal life as we are properly attuned. To me the temple is the good ship *Zion* with Jesus as the Captain. If we stay on board, He will bring us safely home.

I realize that not many will experience being in a small

Jesus the Christ, by Harry Anderson. Drawing of the Salt Lake Temple by Patric Gerber. Courtesy Intellectual Reserve, Inc.

"Come unto me" (Alma 5:35).

boat on a boisterous sea just inches from dangerous waves. All of us, however, by divine design, will experience rough waters, strong winds, and fearful reefs during our voyage through life. Some may seem to have rougher voyages than others, but the truth is, the Lord knows each one of us and tailors experiences for our own eternal good. We must not panic or jump or fall overboard but stay calm, trust our Captain, visit with Him often, do what He says, and believe that He will get us through every danger, both in time and in eternity, which He will.

I have been shaken terribly, engulfed in huge waves, and even thrown into tempestuous seas, yet the Lord has always helped me reach safe harbor. I know that as we stay with Him, He will bring us safely home, whether to a temporary harbor here or an eternal harbor over there.

As I returned from this sacred odyssey, I found myself humming hymns of pleading and praise, as I had done years before and continue to do even now. Yes, "Guide Us, O Thou Great Jehovah." Guide us through this life and through the endless universe beyond—guide us around the danger zones, past the sentinels, and give us the assurance that we are not lost, that Shinehah will rise over there, Olea will be there, Kolob over there, and safe harbor straight ahead.

My gratitude for the Savior, His temple, His universe, and the physical body He has given me (and each of us) knows no bounds. If we go to His house regularly, with great desire to learn from Him and be guided by Him in all things and at all times, we all can know, as I know, that He lives, that He is there—and indeed, that it's all there.

NOTES

CHAPTER 2: THE REAL WORLD

1. Thomas S. Monson, *Teachings of Thomas S. Monson*, comp. Lynne F. Cannegieter (Salt Lake City: Deseret Book, 2011), 78.

CHAPTER 3: PAY ATTENTION!

1. Liz G. Owens wrote the accompanying story in song about this event. I believe she beautifully captures the feelings of not only that moment but of its meaning to all of us.

CHAPTER 7: CHOICES

1. Thomas S. Monson, *Pathways to Perfection: Discourses of Thomas S. Monson* (Salt Lake City: Deseret Book, 1973), 205.

CHAPTER 8: MAKING THE TEMPLE A BIGGER PART OF LIFE

1. Howard W. Hunter, "The Great Symbol of Our Membership," *Ensign*, October 1994, 5.
2. Thomas. S. Monson, "The Holy Temple—a Beacon to the World," *Ensign*, May 2011, 90–94.
3. "Excerpts from Recent Addresses of President Gordon B. Hinckley," *Ensign*, April 1996, 72.

CHAPTER 11: "MY TEMPLE"

1. "I Know That My Redeemer Lives," *Hymns of The Church of Jesus Christ of Latter-day Saints* (Salt Lake City: The Church of Jesus Christ of Latter-day Saints, 1985), no. 136; emphasis added.

CHAPTER 15: MIRACLES AND MYSTERIES

1. "Excerpts from Recent Addresses of President Gordon B. Hinckley," *Ensign*, April 1996, 72.

Chapter 17: Because It Is Right

1. Joseph Smith, *Teachings of the Prophet Joseph Smith,* sel. Joseph Fielding Smith (Salt Lake City: Deseret Book, 1976), 256.

Chapter 21: Mom? Dad?

1. *George Albert Smith,* Teachings of Presidents of the Church series (Salt Lake City: The Church of Jesus Christ of Latter-day Saints, 2011), xxv–xxvi.

Chapter 22: Refuge

1. David O. McKay, in Conference Report, October 1945, 133.

Chapter 24: Cast Your Burdens

1. Chelsie Brown, journal, April 2007; used by permission.
2. James E. Faust, *Ensign,* May 2007, 67–68.
3. Thomas S. Monson, *Teachings of Thomas S. Monson,* comp. Lynne F. Cannegieter (Salt Lake City: Deseret Book, 2011), 79, 78.

Chapter 27: Peace

1. Thomas S. Monson, "The Holy Temple—a Beacon to the World," *Ensign,* May 2011, 93.

Chapter 28: It's All There

1. *David O. McKay,* Teachings of Presidents of the Church series (Salt Lake City: The Church of Jesus Christ of Latter-day Saints, 2003), xxviii.
2. "Jesus, Savior, pilot me / Over life's tempestuous sea" (*Hymns of The Church of Jesus Christ of Latter-day Saints* [Salt Lake City: The Church of Jesus Christ of Latter-day Saints, 1985], no. 104).

   "Master, the tempest is raging! / The billows are tossing high!" (*Hymns,* no. 105).

   "Rock of Ages, cleft for me, / Let me hide myself in thee" (*Hymns,* no. 111).

   "I need thee ev'ry hour, / Most gracious Lord" (*Hymns,* no. 98).

   "Abide with me; 'tis eventide" (*Hymns,* no. 165).

   "Nearer, my God, to thee, / Nearer to thee!" (*Hymns,* no. 100).

   "Jesus, lover of my soul, / Let me to thy bosom fly" (*Hymns,* no. 102).

   "Guide us, O thou great Jehovah, / Guide us to the promised land" (*Hymns,* no. 83).

INDEX